W9-BOB-245

*Forthcoming Volumes in the New
Church's Teaching Series*

The Anglican Vision
James E. Griffiss

Opening the Bible
Roger Ferlo

Engaging the Word
Michael Johnston

The Practice of Prayer
Margaret Guenther

Living with History
Fredrica Harris Thompsett

Early Christian Traditions
Rebecca Lyman

Opening the Prayer Book
Jeffrey D. Lee

Mysteries of Faith
Mark McIntosh

Christian Social Witness
Harold Lewis

Liturgical Prayer
Louis Weil

Ethics After Easter
Stephen Holmgren

Christian Wholeness
Martin L. Smith SSJE

Horizons of Mission
Titus L. Presler

Living with History

The New
Church's Teaching Series
Volume 5

Living with History

Fredrica Harris Thompsett

COWLEY PUBLICATIONS
Cambridge ✦ Boston
Massachusetts

The title *The Church's Teaching Series* is used by permission of the Domestic and Foreign Missionary Society. Use of the series title does not constitute the Society's endorsement of the content of the work.

Library of Congress Cataloging-in-Publication Data:
Thompsett, Fredrica Harris, 1942-
    Living with History / Fredrica Harris Thompsett.
        p.   cm. — (The new church's teaching series; v. 5)
    Includes bibliographical references.
    ISBN 1-56101-160-6 (alk. paper)
    ✓ 1. Episcopal Church—History. 2. Church of England—History. 3. Anglican Communion—United States—History. I. Title. II. Series.
BX5880.T47 1998
283'.09—dc21
                                                    98-47077
                                                    CIP

Cynthia Shattuck, editor; Vicki Black, copyeditor and designer

This book is printed on recycled, acid-free paper and was produced in Canada.

Cowley Publications • 28 Temple Place
Boston, Massachusetts 02111
800-225-1534 • www.cowley.org

Table of Contents

The New Church's Teaching Series

Almost fifty years ago a series for the Episcopal Church called The Church's Teaching was launched with the publication of Robert Dentan's *The Holy Scriptures* in 1949. Again in the 1970s the church commissioned another church's teaching series for the next generation of Anglicans. Originally the series was part of an effort to give the growing postwar churches a sense of Anglican identity: what Anglicans share with the larger Christian community and what makes them distinctive within it. During that seemingly more tranquil era it may have been easier to reach a consensus and to speak authoritatively. Now, at the end of the twentieth century, consensus and authority are more difficult; there is considerably more diversity of belief and practice within the churches today, and more people than ever who have never been introduced to the church at all.

The books in this new teaching series for the Episcopal Church attempt to encourage and respond to the times—and to the challenges that will usher out the old century and bring in the new. This new series differs from the previous two in significant ways: it has no official status, claims no special authority, speaks in a personal voice, and comes not out of committees but from scholars and pastors meeting and talking informally together. It assumes a different readership: adults who are not "cradle Anglicans," but who come from other religious traditions or from no tradition at all, and who want to know what Anglicanism has to offer.

As the series editor I want to thank E. Allen Kelley, former president of Morehouse Publishing, for initially inviting me to bring together a group of teachers and pastors who could write with learning and conviction about their faith. I am grateful both to him and to Morehouse for participating in the early development of the series.

Since those initial conversations there have been changes in the series itself, but its basic purpose has remained: to explore the themes of the Christian life through Holy Scripture, historical and contemporary theology, worship, spirituality, social witness, ethics, and mission. It is our hope that all readers, Anglicans and otherwise, will find the books an aid in their continuing growth into Christ.

James E. Griffiss
Series Editor

Acknowledgments

In *Northanger Abbey*, Jane Austen's most satirical novel, the heroine remarks that she finds history tiresome: "The quarrels of popes and kings...the men all so good for nothing; and hardly any women at all." Clearly something was missing! At its best, history offers glimpses into the holiness of people's everyday lives. This history book provides an opportunity to reflect on people and parishes, faith and friendship among both women and men.

So too people and parishes, long ago and close at hand, have shaped what is written here. I still carry lessons learned in my youth at Christ Church Cranbrook in Bloomfield Hills, Michigan. More recently, a Lenten study group at Christ Episcopal Church in Needham, Massachusetts engaged my questions about tradition and change in the Episcopal Church with good humor, curiosity, and memorable insights. My current parish—Saint Barnabas Memorial Church, Falmouth, Massachusetts—and its rector, Robert B. Appleyard, Jr., have sustained and challenged me anew, Sunday by Sunday.

Along the way I have sought and gained much from the good company of historians and other scholars. I am particularly indebted to Mary Donovan, Gardiner Shattuck, Edward Rodman, and Ellen Wondra for their advice and counsel. Scott Paradise, former chaplain at the Massachusetts Institute of Technology, encouraged me to examine the ecological crisis through the lens of an Anglican historian. Collectively, members of the Episcopal Women's History Project continue to expand my historical vision. I hold two senior scholars in highest regard for their abiding wisdom: John Booty, my faculty predecessor in Church History at the Episcopal Divinity School; and Verna Dozier, irrepressible friend and prophetic biblical teacher.

A younger generation of EDS students and scholars—Susan Ackley, Matthew Cadwell, and Sarah Eastman—served energetically as research assistants. Their labors were funded by grants from the Theological Writing Fund at EDS and by the Episcopal Church's Conant Fund. The current faculty of EDS, whose patience I have surely tried as I repeatedly sought their assistance, were unerringly helpful and generous, as were other members of the student body, staff, and administration. With all of this assistance and support, any errors and omissions, that may remain in this volume, are of my own making.

As this book has taken shape, in my home life I have grieved over the deaths of close family members, young and old, thankfully witnessed Dorothy Brittain's courageous recovery from illness, and welcomed daily assistance from Charlene Higbe. In all, I am fortunate to know God's love in the holiness of friendship, people, and parishes, old and new.

Fredrica Harris Thompsett

Chapter One

Living with History

My father was an avid reader of historical biographies—the bigger and heavier the better, or so it seemed to me as a child. I once asked him why he so enjoyed reading about the life and times of other people, and in reply he invited me to share his enthusiasm for history. On my next birthday two gifts appeared, purchased during one of his frequent trips to England. One was a cloth doll, in full sixteenth-century costume, of Queen Elizabeth I. I have this elegantly clothed and much-beloved doll to this day. The other was a short paperback book entitled, if memory serves me well, *The Little Princesses*, which told me about the childhood of Elizabeth and Margaret Rose, daughters of the reigning English king at that time, George VI. These historical gifts provided me with many hours of fanciful musing about the lives and times of two women monarchs: the famous Tudor Queen Elizabeth I who helped establish the Church of England, and the young woman who one day would be crowned Queen Elizabeth II. I was hooked on both history and biography. My father was not surprised—only bemused—when later on I decided to study English history in graduate school.

Our sense of history is frequently homegrown: home is its starting point. My youthful enthusiasm for the life and times of English queens was not an isolated interest, but an important point of departure. I was not collecting this or that treasured relic as an antiquarian or hobbyist might. Rather, I was absorbed in learning about various aspects of the lives of people, living and dead, who caught my interest in the present: princesses and pageantry, women and leadership, Christians and the majesty of religious life. Through my study of history I came to know the power of a good story.

Many of us are drawn to certain questions, images, and figures because they say something about our identity. *What* we choose to notice says something about *who* we are today. Living with history involves making choices about what to recall, what to remember. Yet history does not stop at home. It is a collective community enterprise that involves broadening our understanding of humanity beyond our immediate family and local circumstances. When history is sensitively constructed, it is neither narrowly parochial nor limited in vision. Knowledge of history invites us to know other peoples and ages, to test our assumptions alongside the experiences of those of diverse languages, cultures, and races from different times. Such multicultural remembering can contribute to building up a shared understanding and tolerance among peoples. Recalling times of plenty and times of hardship can illumine our futures, offering consolation as well as hope. With the clarity of historical perspective, we can also temper the arrogance of our present-mindedness, shedding new light on problems we had thought were ours alone. Looking backward widens our vision, displaying the achievements, struggles, failures, and wisdom of other ages. Like Chaucer's medieval tales of a fair field full of folk assembled to go on pilgrimage, the tapestry of church history presents a diverse panorama of spirit-filled people endeavoring—though not always succeeding—to remain in faithful relation with one another and with God.

History is about remembering. It centers on calling to mind persons, events, and themes that have meaning for our lives. The "story" part of hi*story* is built over time as each generation passes on to the next generation the selective memory of influential persons, major turning points, and occasions of marked joy or tragedy. Of course, not all of us are good at remembering, and we therefore think we are not good at history. But what does it mean to have a "good" memory? Many of us worry about our memories, especially as we grow old. Mark Twain once quipped, "When I was young I could remember anything, whether it happened or not." Some of us have a hard time remembering numbers. I am often, for example, called up short when asked to recite my Social Security number, and I admit that, even as a historian, recalling the date of this or that event remains a challenge. I know that others share this struggle to remember.

Yet learning about history is *not* primarily about memorizing one date after another. We do not have to remember things that we can look up: I can write down my Social Security number. I tell new students of church history about dictionaries and other resources where they can look up historical information, such as *The Oxford Dictionary of the Christian Church*. I use this text like a historical Webster's dictionary, looking up accurate information on names, dates, and concepts, as well as correct spellings. Some adult learners, especially those who like to visualize events century by century, enjoy looking at books with historical timelines in which various categories of information—politics, economics, religion, diplomacy, science, the arts, and so on—are portrayed horizontally across each century. We have our own systems for remembering. There is no one right way to remember history: we can use whatever method works best for each one of us.

I think having a "good" memory is actually about being able to recall persons, places, and images that have significance for us. Memory is unerringly selective, both in terms of what we struggle to memorize and what we are eventually able to recall. History is not about citing one neutral fact or uninteresting date after another, but about sharing stories that hold meaning for us, whether their lessons are for good or ill. Most of us can remember the faces of beloved family members, even those long deceased. In these recollections, when our memories dim we are often aided by looking at cherished photographs or old mementos. Shortly after my father's death, my family and I gathered around an old photo album and each of us recounted episodes in my father's life somewhat differently, according to our own perspective. My young nephews listened with delight and good humor as a fuller history of their grandfather's life and times emerged. In effect we were biographers, writing out loud an important part of our family history, as well as passing it on to the younger generations in our midst.

∼ Begin with Questions

A good way to begin learning history is to ask lots of questions. One of the first questions to ask when we are reading history is, who is the author? What are her or his special interests? What community is he writing from? What community is she writing to? Observing where a historian begins and ends can provide important clues. What does he or she choose to notice? It is also a good idea to think about not only who is present, but who is missing or absent from this historical account. Are women involved as well as men? And where are the children, the servants, the elderly, and those who are poor? Whose testimonies are given the most weight? Am I challenged by this historian to discover what I really think? Many of these questions resemble those involved in studying the scriptures; in this sense, studying history is similar to studying the Bible. Reading church history, like searching the scriptures, invites diligent readers to ask questions about the past and to reclaim wisdom for the future.

Asking questions is also central to the way historians work: the more questions we ask, the more possibilities come to mind. I like to imagine historians as persistent young children pursuing a fascinating tale. The telling of the story is punctuated by numerous inquiries: "What happened next? Why? Why not? Who was there? Who was not?" Posing these and other pressing questions moves the story along and shapes the focus for research. Pointed curiosity guides historians' inquiries as they identify and explore familiar sources as well as uncover new information. Following the story where it leads is part of the labor and the discipline of being a historian. Given the passions, preferences, and questions that historians bring to the choice of subjects for their work, what matters is that historians are guided by the evidence they discover. The craft of history is scientific as well as intuitive. Assessments of past events need to be supported by diligent and thoughtful research. Scholarship and discipline are involved, as well as faithful crafting of interpretations that speak to us in the present.

As we undertake any study of history, it is important to pay attention to the words we use, for they can tell us much about the people who used them. The term *Anglicanism*, for example, has a history. Historically, the adjective "Anglican" dates from the 1630s, while written use of the term "Anglicanism" first appeared in the 1830s. Today historians use this term to represent an understanding of Christian faith and practice as it evolved in England during the Reformation and in succeeding centuries. Contemporary Episcopalians often use this term more broadly to describe our English religious past, referring to the "faith, practice, and spirit" of churches of the Anglican Communion.[1] As the Anglican Communion becomes increasingly multicultural, the term "Anglicanism" no longer means a particularly English expression of the Christian faith. Thus, as the Anglican church has changed and evolved over the centuries, the words used to describe it have had to adapt and change as well.

I have emphasized that reading history is personal, and that knowledge of history does not keep us stuck in the past. Actually, the desire to learn from the past is born in the present. Historical knowledge can free us to face the future with fresh perspectives and renewed hope. Jane Dempsey Douglas, a modern historian of the Reformation era, once described historians as those who have to back up one thousand years in order to get a running start on the present! Since the historical character of Christianity is a given, generations upon generations of our ancestors have found that looking backward promotes thinking forward.

A prime example of this use of historical knowledge in Anglicanism is the way our sixteenth-century Reformation ancestors reclaimed their understanding of Christian tradition. Those responsible for shaping the Reformation in England turned for wisdom and authoritative guidance to scripture, to biblical images of the church, and to the early councils and creeds. They enthusiastically built upon one of the great gifts of the Renaissance, a high regard for the past. By giving prominence first to scriptural accounts and then to the experience of the early Christian communities, particularly those in the first five centuries of the church's life, these researchers of historical texts endeavored to restore in England a church that was faithful to the gospel in its leadership, worship, and daily living. Tradition served for them as both a starting point and a constituent element informing new beliefs and patterns of action. With the authoritative tools of scripture, reason, *and* tradition, they hoped to conserve, independent of the papacy, the best of Catholic life and faith. Like other Protestant reformers, they sought to ground the life and worship of their church in the revealed truth of Holy Scripture. In essence, our illustrious Reformation ancestors backed up one thousand years to the traditions of their forebears in order to respond to the questions and challenges of their own day.

In much the same way for Anglicans in the last few years of this millennium, living with history means living with changes in our traditions: disruptions in our sense of how things are, how they have always been in the past, and how they ought to be in the future. As our historical story unfolds, we must ask questions about our own sense of tradition and how we are to live with so many aspects of our religious life in flux, for the traditions we uphold tell us who we are and where we have come from. Like our sense of history, our sense of tradition is homegrown.

∽ Tradition Begins at Home

In my imagination church buildings are seldom empty. They are filled with family and friends, beloved faces from many generations. This is especially true of parishes where I have belonged. Even today when I walk into the parish in which I was raised as a child, I am transported back to the early 1950s. We are sitting with my mother in her usual pew, my brother squirming while I have my head down reading the prayer book. As my mind lingers, I see and indeed hear others. There is the much-beloved Director of Religious Education, Diantha, whose embracing, British-accented voice drew many of us into the bosom of the church. It was Diantha who first encouraged me, at the age of eight, to "be a teacher," by helping out in the church school. Over there is my mother's best friend, Dean, a strikingly tall, dramatic woman who always had a kind word for me, while the founders and benefactors of this parish, the Booths, sat in a pew up front on the left. When on our parish anniversary we would sing "The Church's One Foundation," I *knew* who the founders were!

On the first Sunday of the month we had a communion service. I would look for Diantha, for Dean, for the Booths, and for others I knew and loved as members of the congregation came forward to receive Holy Communion. Religion as a whole for me—church, communion, worshiping God—was bathed in the incarnate light of familiar faces. This was, of course, not the whole story, but it was a good starting place. The smell and sight of the sanctuary, the setting of the altar, the vestments, the orderly lighting of the candles by young acolytes, the sounds of the senior choir, and all those cherished things we did together as a parish: these habits and customs meant "church" to me. Church was what we actually *did* together: the singing, the movement, the actions, and the processions. I was confident that we were doing exactly what we were supposed to do and that each and every parish church was more or less like mine.

I suspect that all of us who have spent any time in churches as children have strong memories of people we loved, songs we liked to sing, customs we cherished. Those who were not raised in the church may have their own memories of family religious traditions. These memories comprise the beginning of our religious autobiographies:

faces, traditions, sights, smells, sounds, and tastes that are all part of our individual histories. Some of our memories are pleasant and comforting; others are troubling, and can keep us from entering more deeply into church life as adults. The only mildly uncomfortable memory I have is my struggle with trying to sit still in that hard pew during the long Communion Sunday service—and I still have an axiomatic aversion to services that last much longer than an hour. For me, an hour or so is "traditional." It was the way I was raised, the length I believed church services were supposed to be.

The fact that change happens was taken for granted in just about every aspect of my childhood except one: I never expected my beloved church to change. It was not until I was a teenager that I received my first hints of the bewildering diversity and potential for change in parish life and practice. As often happens in Anglican churches, the liturgy was the vehicle and focus for the changes. One day my mother, a representative from our parish to the local diocesan conventions in the late 1950s, returned from one such meeting fuming about liturgical change. It was all right, she said, that "they"—faceless religious authorities—wanted to modernize prayer book language, but it was not all right that they wanted to change and even omit particular phrases she cherished. No, it was not the new wording for the Lord's Prayer or the Twenty-third Psalm that bothered her, as it later did so many. Together Mother and I looked up one of her favorite phrases. It occurred in the General Confession when the congregation prayed, "Have mercy upon us, miserable offenders." For her the phrase "miserable offenders" carried special meaning, not because she was generally miserable—far from it. Indeed, she was a rather dramatic, upbeat, and breezy person! Yet at some deep level, through regular, customary usage of this confession, these words had caught her attention and grounded her sense of penitence. At such a time she knew herself truly to be a "miserable offender." "No experts," she told me, "will take away *my* prayer." I have not forgotten what I learned from her about the value of our capacity for deep, personal investment in religious language and customs.

One other experience opened my eyes to the surprising diversity of Episcopal churches in the 1950s. As a member of a national youth choir and orchestra, I traveled on tour my senior year in high school. We journeyed from Michigan to Texas. There, with a new teenage boyfriend who came from Dallas, I had my first experience of the sights and sounds, smells and bells of what has been called "high church" or Anglo-Catholic ritual and tradition. Everything in the liturgy seemed new and confusing to me. I did not know the signals about when we were to kneel or stand, let alone to "cross ourselves" or genuflect. The vestments were new to me, some of the prayers were unfamiliar, and songs were sung in odd places. Lonely and far away from home, I had expected on a Sunday morning to share a comforting sense of tradition with my new friend. Instead, I felt awkward and out of place. The impact of these changes, of finding the unfamiliar in the very place where I longed for the familiar, created a sense of disappointment and loss. The faith of my mothers and fathers seemed far, far away.

I eventually learned that those of us who called ourselves Protestants typically came from parishes whose traditions and customs emphasized the "low church," reformed character of our faith. Conversely, "high church" parishes tended to emphasize and have more in common with traditional Catholic practices and sensibilities. Today an even wider range of diversity in liturgical styles can be found in the same state and diocese, even among parishes in the same town. Yet people who are new to the Episcopal Church, as well as those who have spent most of their lives in one parish, can still be surprised by practices that differ markedly from the first church they ever knew. Our most passionately held understandings of religious traditions are formed as we worship, whether in common prayer or in our private meditations. One way of understanding tradition is to see it as *the accumulated product of experiences that have long, continued usage.* I have shared reminiscences from my own childhood here not because my own upbringing was in any way unusual, but to emphasize how personal preferences and experience in prayer are foundational in shaping our commitments to religious traditions and customs.

Imagine, for a moment, your own local parish church *without* the familiar traditions and practices you cherish most. If you think you would be disappointed and upset, if not angered, by changes great and small, you would not be alone. Changes in traditional worship patterns, customs, and language have been the norm and not the exception for most Christians in the second half of the twentieth century. The fact is that the churches of the Christian west—including Roman Catholic, Lutheran, Presbyterian, and Methodist, as well as Episcopal—have been and are living through a period of widespread change in the form of liturgical revision: changing the way worship is conducted. When Episcopalians officially approved and replaced the 1928 *Book of Common Prayer* with the 1979 version, we were part of a wider ecumenical movement—after which few (if any) congregations looked or acted like the parish I grew up in during the 1950s.

ᴥ Returning to Our Roots

Paradoxically, this movement for liturgical change has over the long haul brought us into closer touch with our earliest traditions. When communities are asked to embrace the new, they often respond by going back to their roots. At such times longstanding traditions are examined and held up to the light of new scholarship and insight, as they are reviewed with an eye to their present utility and effectiveness. This process of assessing the present and of repossessing long-held traditions involves looking both forward and backward. At such times churches not only reflect on what they are doing now, but also look back to formative periods and persons from the past. Anglicans naturally look to the English Reformation and specifically to the primary author of our first prayer books, Thomas Cranmer. As a historian of the English Reformation, I look also to the formative theologian and apologist Richard Hooker, who at the end of the sixteenth century summed up and explicated the theological foundations for the church's ministry and organization. In the same way, Lutherans in the process of revision and change naturally look to the writings of Martin Luther, while the first few centuries of the church's life (the "patristic period," or time of the church fathers) provide all Christians with formative shapes and patterns of worship. At the end of our own century, after taking a fresh look at the past, we may be closer to the intentions of our earliest Christian ancestors than we were at the start.

Most of us like to think of ourselves as forward-looking and broadminded, especially given the comprehensive character of Anglican life and practice. Yet many of us also dislike change in the church, which is the last place we expect or want to see it. When much else seems to be changing, uncertain, or perhaps adrift in our societal and personal lives, many of us want the church, the ground and source of our faith, to remain the same. This is understandable, indeed laudable, but can it ever be achieved?

Church history is replete with the stories of those who have attempted to preserve stability in times of flux by going back to fundamentals. They make lists of the core beliefs and doctrines of Christianity. The fifth-century monk Vincent of Lerins identified as criteria for true Catholic faith those tenets of faith that were "believed everywhere, always, and by all." Contemporary Anglicans take a different tack. If I were to list basic affirmations that Christians hold in common, my list would include the grounding of Christian truth in the scriptures, the humanity and divinity of Christ, the relational and triune nature of God, and the efficacy of the sacraments of baptism and eucharist. It is clear to me, however, that not only will our lists of "core beliefs" differ, the interpretation of individual items will vary even more.

Think, on one hand, about the debates that have always raged over the interpretation of scripture and about differing understandings of Christology: who *is* the Christ for Christians today? Committed and sincere Christians continue to disagree on such important matters. Interpreting, explaining, and illustrating beliefs in the language of the day is the primary task that has put theologians to work throughout the ages. Even Vincent of Lerins left the door open for doctrinal development as the truth of scripture became more fully explicated. Substantial disagreement among believers is neither new nor particularly contemporary. Christian beginnings were far from homogenous; Paul's response to those disputing factions among the Corinthians is a case in point. Debate is inevitable among those who seek after truth. Indeed, our God is known to reveal truths hidden from prior generations, as well as to do new things in this and other ages. Who would expect a fixed or closed system from a God who promises to make all things new?

Yet sincere questions about tradition and change still persist. For example, one young mother worries that with all the changes taking place in contemporary society, how can she be sure that tradition is "alive and well" in her church? A lawyer wonders whether we can address today's issues honestly and remain true to the traditional faith; another asks bluntly, "What if the church is wrong?" One old-timer dislikes the fact that controversies and conflicts in his denomination make front-page news. He asks, "Why can't the church go back to the good old days, when it never rocked the boat?" Some people claim there are far too many changes for the "older people" to tolerate, yet ironically many elders speak of liking change: they welcome new customs to their congregation. And all these are part of a larger question: *How does tradition inform and shape our continuing witness as contemporary Christians?*

∿ Tradition, Traditions, and Traditionalists

Tradition is not an endangered species. It has been around a long time, so long that we have developed several different meanings for the same term. My Webster's dictionary gives three, each with a religious aspect. The first is "the handing down of information, beliefs, and customs by word of mouth or by example from one generation to another without written instruction." Here tradition is oral information that is valuable enough for a community to preserve and pass on, such as the instructions in Deuteronomy to pass on God's commandments to "your children and your children's children" (6:2).

Second, tradition is "an inherited, established, or customary pattern of thought, action, or behavior (as a religious practice or a social custom)," which is the most common use in the church; it refers to that which is handed down. Tradition is actually many things, a large and expansive concept that encompasses the creeds, early Christian teaching, liturgical worship, and established patterns of institutional and spiritual life. Tradition here refers to that which is inherited and based on long, continued usage. Third and last, tradition is "cultural continuity in social attitudes and institutions." When we speak of a person or institution as expressing "traditional viewpoints," we are describing continuity rather than novelty.

It is important to note that each of these meanings is active, dynamic: each is about communication and movement. Both the Greek and Latin words for "tradition" convey this sense of activity. The Greek word Paul uses to speak of delivering the news of Christ's redemptive acts is *paradosi*: "For I handed on to you as of first importance what I in turn had received" (1 Corinthians 15:3). The Latin equivalent is *traditio*, the active process of "handing over" information. I know it is not grammatically correct, but I prefer to think of "tradition" as a verb—a living activity and not a static object. We, the everyday believers, are active agents in the process of "traditioning"—carrying and handing on living tradition—as we experience and express our faith. Each age of believers has tellers of the story, bearers of the customs, shapers of the liturgies, poets, and seekers who together deliver and hand on tradition. Each of us who learns and passes on the story is a "traditionalist." And I am proud to be one too! This does not mean I am necessarily a conservative, although as a historian of the church and an everyday believer I often look backward. Rather, it means that, like other baptized Christians, I intend, in the words of the Baptismal Covenant, to "continue in the apostles' teaching and fellowship, and in the prayers."

Christian theologians also speak of *the* Tradition with a capital "T." This is not, as some of us may suspect, a summative term for all primary beliefs or the early creeds, or even for prayer book worship. The Tradition is Jesus Christ. In this sense there is only one Tradition. When we proclaim the gospel of Christ and vigorously pass on Christian teaching we are engaging the Tradition. Some theologians speak of this as the core doctrine; the Greek word here is *kerygma,* gospel preaching. We convey the Tradition through our expression of tradition, and church historians listen to and learn from those of other ages who have labored to express the Tradition as they shaped the traditions of their day. For me this also means recovering voices that have been ignored, silenced, or trivialized in other statements of tradition. Thus, for example, I sometimes labor to find and hear the voices of women in the midst of biblical and historical materials. There are numerous ways in which Christian scholars still learn from looking backward, reforming, renewing, correcting, and expanding our knowledge of significant revelatory events and movements. Tradition, as I noted earlier, is a large and expansive category.

What comes to mind when we think about the faith we express as "tradition"? For many Christians the three creeds—the Apostles' Creed, the Nicene Creed, and the Athanasian Creed—are important statements of basic beliefs. The story of our early Christian ancestors' struggles to shape these historic documents is recorded in another volume in this teaching series. Today Episcopalians use the Apostles' Creed in baptism, and the Nicene Creed is part of our eucharistic services. These documents authoritatively proclaim the nature of God as three persons, as the Trinity.

Does this mean for Episcopalians that the creeds have a more important place in our understanding of the Tradition? The best response is a qualified yes: the creeds are a normative part of our written tradition and carry considerable weight not because they were written down so early in the church's life, nor because of the consensus they have achieved in centuries of use, but because, as one scholar writes, "they accord with the basic prophetic and apostolic testimony."[2] Does this mean they can be replaced? No: whether they continue to be used in worship or not, their status as historic, received documents is established.

Indeed, continuity and change alike are traditional components for framing Anglican worship. The very first sentence of the first *Book of Common Prayer*, approved for use in 1549 and largely drafted by Thomas Cranmer, asserts:

> There was never any thing by the wit of man so well devised, or so sure established, which in continuance of time hath not been corrupted: as, among other things, it may plainly appear by the common prayers in the Church. (BCP 866)

Cranmer's belief that from age to age churches would need to change and reorder their liturgies, their "common prayers," was prophetic. Only three years later, in 1552, Cranmer was influential in drafting a radically revised prayer book, and further revisions would follow in 1559, 1662, and so on to the present.

Plainly, liturgical change is itself an expected part of Anglican tradition. Indeed, this is the conclusion of the most definitive Anglican statement we have "Of the Traditions of the Church," found in the Articles of Religion, sometimes called the Thirty-Nine Articles. These statements, first drafted by Cranmer, were revised and adopted in 1563. Article XXXIV states:

It is not necessary that Traditions and Ceremonies be in all places one, or utterly like; for at all times they have been divers, and may be changed according to the diversity of countries, times, and men's manners. (BCP 874)

With the confident rhetoric of a new Republic, the preface to the first *Book of Common Prayer* adopted for use in the United States in 1789 appeals to expediency and "the liberty wherewith Christ hath made us free" as valid reasons for change in public worship.

ᴗ Can Anything New Be True?

Certain axioms prevail in institutional church life, from "How it used to be is how it should remain" to the mocking hymn refrain I once heard, "Nothing new can be true!" Folks do not always come right out and say such things, but they are appealing to the past as a fixed object as the basis for their stance. Sometimes they simply respond to change with, "We've never done it that way before." There is a clear popular assumption that upholding tradition is one sure way to prohibit change, yet assumptions about "how things used to be" frequently are inaccurate or incomplete.

Sometimes popular traditions survive today only as fragments. I think of the past as another country, a place where a different language of primary assumptions is spoken and lived. One brief example of the fragmentary nature of our knowledge of history is the church ritual that survives only in an odd phrase about "bringing home the bacon." This saying dates from a twelfth-century English church contest where a prize was awarded to any married man who could solemnly swear he had not quarreled with his wife for a year and a day. The winner took home a side of bacon. My point is not that tradition is trivial, but rather that it is the record of the church's decisions through time, including its errors and irrelevancies.

A deeper and more complete understanding of history refutes the popularly held notions that tradition is the substance of things that do not change, and that tradition in the church is immutable. One mistake we often make is arrogantly equating the present time with the full measure of truth. This clinging to the present is just as idolatrous as ossifying the past: it lets only today define what is possible. Another fallacy in declaring tradition as the symbol of things that do not change is apparent in our limited, partial comprehension of divine intentions. As receivers and bearers of the Tradition, Christians carry responsibility both for preserving historic hallmarks of the faith and also for responding to God's actions in our midst. Bishop Richard Holloway explains it this way:

> Our God does new things, does things for the first time, reveals truths hidden from previous generations and made known only unto us in these last days. The danger and paradox of our faith is that a too unyielding loyalty to the truths of our tradition can end as a disloyalty to the living God by whom previous generations were prodded into new truth.[3]

The Bible is full of the voices of prophets urging us to notice the new, to interrupt the familiar and break through established patterns of estrangement. Martin Smith of the Society of St. John the Evangelist recently noted in a public lecture that one definition of sin is "the willful refusal to conceive something new and different." We need not abandon the past to imagine the new and the different, but the conversation between past and present has to continue.

There is one other strategy for resisting change that is familiar to those of us living in perplexing, bewildering times: the appeal to a "golden age" in the past. Most of those who turn with nostalgia to such an epoch are referring to persons who, in their own time, were nostalgic about yet another golden age. In a New York subway station, I recently observed this colorful example of graffiti: "Nostalgia is not what it used to be...and never was!" Each age has something to teach us: all peoples and cultures, including those that differ markedly from our own. Nostalgia stops us from getting real about the past; it cuts us off from tradition. The desire to return to a golden age is often grounded in the mistaken notion that sameness and relative peacefulness are normative for Christians. Bishop Holloway calls this "the tranquillist heresy," a phrase I like. In my own life, as in my study of history, I have found that controversies born of differing factions and strongly contended points of view are recognizable and inescapable components of searching for the truth. The Tradition is anything but static; the gospel is dynamic, and we struggle to express and live out this truth in ways that are never completely settled. Controversy is part of the life of faith, bringing energy and making room for the future.

Taking time to consider the impact of controversy and change in our lives, as well as in our denominational family, is a challenge fraught with difficulty. Richard Hooker observed at the end of the sixteenth century that change is not made without inconvenience, even when we are moving from worse to better. There are different occasions and pressures for change. Some things of ancient use prove to be harmful in the present day; some practices are determined to be no longer convenient or helpful, while still others are called forth in response to new occasions. In each of these, Hooker notes, change is accompanied by protests of inconvenience, even when we are moving from worse to better.[4]

The economic and social institution of chattel slavery, to take one dramatic example, was received and sanctioned by the framers of America's Constitution as they were forming a democratic nation. Over time the human devastation of slavery was increasingly weighed against texts from the Bible urging obedience and submission to masters (see 1 Timothy 6:1 and Titus 2:9), while other texts throwing the practice of slavery into question (like Paul's words in Galatians 3, "there is no longer slave or free") took on new significance. Eventually the institution of chattel slavery was reevaluated and overthrown: the traditional understandings had to change.

Other traditions need to be changed because they are no longer convenient or useful. For example, setting the worship of the church in the language of the people was a distinct accomplishment during the English Reformation, although many protested against this change and grieved the loss of the Latin liturgy, just as some Roman Catholics who prefer the Latin mass do today. Sometimes church customs, initiated for other reasons long ago, take on associations of holiness and sanctity. One such long familiar matter of contention among Anglicans is the question of when to stand, kneel, or sit in the liturgy. For example, it is said that we have "always" knelt at the altar to receive Holy Communion. Not so: altar rails were first instituted at the end of the sixteenth century, not for pious reasons but to keep dogs and perhaps even cattle out of the way. Once rails surrounded the altar, some clergy began to suggest communicants might come forward rather than following the traditional practice of taking the elements out into the church to communicate the poor who were standing and those who could afford a seat (or, in later centuries, who could rent a pew). Whatever devotional reasons were associated with kneeling to receive communion, historically it is a short-lived custom. Today the "tradition" in parishes varies: some kneel, others stand, and sometimes both patterns exist in the same congregation. In actual use this custom is becoming an incidental rather than an essential practice. The English reformers spoke of "things indifferent," *adiaphora*, to distinguish those areas where Christians have the freedom to choose.

Anglican perspectives on change also allow us to address new occasions whereby a long-established tradition is reevaluated in the light of scripture and reason. When we say we are guided in decision-making by scripture, reason, and tradition, it means that we turn to several sources of wisdom. Some of the other resources for problem solving that we typically bring to the table when we are faced with challenges to tradition and disputes about change include what we are learning from current experience, the use of our imagination, continued questioning, and new scientific discoveries. These and other sources of wisdom work best in relationship rather than trying to play off one component against another, as if appeals to scripture, reason, and tradition were in competition. Instead, each has a distinctive and interrelated role.

Recognizing the need for change and upholding tradition are not antithetical intentions. Passing on tradition involves taking risks, since we are, as Hooker noticed, inconvenienced by change. Some changes are harder for us to accept than others, and changes that are hurtful or limiting to some may be the cause of rejoicing and new life for others. At my mother's memorial service, I saw to it that we used the "old" language of the General Confession, recalling her beloved "miserable offenders" phrase into our prayerful midst. I like to think that today my mother would be amused and delighted to know that one of my favorite groups of church musicians is called The Miserable

Offenders. When it comes to contemplating changes that inevitably lie ahead of us in our parishes and throughout the wider church, I find it best to respect those who hold differing perspectives, while recalling my mother's frequent advice, "Never say never."

Throughout the rest of this book, my focus will be on looking backward in order to move forward. I wish to rediscover and conserve lessons from Anglican history that will give us sustenance and continuity in a new millennium, when our children and their children will experience changes in their lifetimes that we have not anticipated. As they renew and reform the church of their day, what traditions might we want them to conserve? What achievements, what hard-fought lessons learned from the collective biographies of our ancestors have brought us this far on the way? What guidance from the past continues to embolden us to go out and do the work we are given to do?

In the next chapter I will continue to look at the historian's task by highlighting ten of the remarkable achievements in our history that I think have formed who we are at this point. These ten achievements, or "touchstones," are examples of a broad, thematic approach to history. In subsequent chapters we will explore a few of these touchstones more deeply through the historical methods of storytelling, biography, and analysis. In chapter three the subject of ministry will be central—particularly the role of the laity in the life of the church, which is a topic too often neglected in church history. In recent years we have moved beyond traditional understandings of church leadership, with an increased focus on lay ministries. What traditions supported and encouraged this change? What promise for future decision-making does this development hold?

In chapter four I will look at Anglicanism and conflict, exploring some ways in which the church has dealt with conflict by compromising with it, ignoring it, or embracing it, to see what lessons we can learn for the present. In chapter five, I want to explore how it is possible to "recycle" traditional theological understandings in order to reclaim customs, practices, and theological perspectives that will help us in the present. The practice of ecology, for example, is both a metaphor and a present-day reality through which we can evaluate our spirituality of creation and support a healthier world. I will conclude this book by suggesting principles and directions for claiming new life as part of our customary identity, as well as for assuring that tradition continues to thrive faithfully in the church of the future.

Chapter Two

Ten Touchstones of History

When a new year begins, opinion makers in newspapers, magazines, television, and now on the Internet typically take on the challenge of naming a "top ten" list in this or that category. Teams and sports events, novels and movies, economic trends and commercial fads are listed, scored, and promoted as "the greatest influence" of the year. The same kind of stock-taking occurs on a larger scale when one decade or one century passes into another. Historians, journalists, and other public commentators recall outstanding achievements, tragedies, and turning points, and assess their impact. The beginning of a new millennium is obviously an important time for taking stock. It is not surprising that as the first millennium turned toward the second, Christian monks, who were among the chroniclers of the European middle ages, commented on past events and boldly listed portents yet to come. Their predictions about the future tended to be less successful than their assessments of the past, but that is not the point. By reading their historical accounts, we are able to discover what they valued enough to preserve and what they hoped would continue.

This kind of focused remembering is also part of the heritage of the people of God. Our biblical ancestors were inclined to make lists of great events and people; that is how they remembered those who had gone before them. Thus the author of the book of Ecclesiasticus begins a paean to the illustrious leaders of former times with the invitation, "Let us now sing the praises," and goes on to enumerate those who were the rich and famous in their own day (44:1). Matthew's gospel likewise begins with lists—not only of Jesus' genealogy and ancestors, but also Jesus' list of the blessed, calling to mind the meek, the poor, the bereaved, the merciful, the peacemakers, those who hunger and thirst for God's righteousness, and those who are persecuted (5:3-12). The Beatitudes is obviously a very different list from the one in Ecclesiasticus, with a different purpose in mind, but both are inspired and impassioned calls to remember. Both appear to be designed at least in part for edification, for building up people of faith and strengthening their commitment to God. Similarly, reading about the church's history is an adventure that invites our enthusiastic response and continuing participation.

In this chapter I would like to follow their example by naming ten key touchstones that I would place on a "top ten" list in the history of the church. What achievements and beliefs do we choose to pass on from this generation to the next? If we were asked to picture the major events and achievements of our lives, what would be included in our family album? This exercise will give us a close-up view of how historians work, particularly of how they select what they will study and reveal about history from the perspective of their own interests and passions. In chapter one we learned something about the historian's task in making sense of the relationship between history, tradition, and change. Here we will explore how things in the distant and not-so-distant past influence and form us today.

The result is my own "personal best" list, grounded in my heritage as a Christian, as an American, as a member of the Anglican Communion who lives and works in the United States, and as a committed, lifelong Episcopalian. Once again we see historical selectivity at work—not only my own personal perspective, but also my social, cultural, ecclesiastical, and geographical vantage point. I begin with three touchstones from the lives of our biblical ancestors that continue to affect us today, and then jump to the sixteenth century and two foundational achievements from the English Reformation, a particularly formative period for Anglicans. The remaining five touchstones are part of the history of the Episcopal Church in the United States.

The following "top ten" come with an invitation and a challenge. I invite you to read through this list, noticing what catches your attention. How would you change this list, extending it and making it your own? What events in your life, in your reading of history, and in your understanding of faithful living have informed your identity as a believer? You might begin by naming one valued ancestor or achievement. Others may well follow. Above all my intent is to invite you to draw insight from the past, to highlight knowledge that will refresh and embolden our continuing perceptions of what matters in the present.

∽ 1. Called into Covenant

Theology typically begins with a desire to understand God. Similarly, the study of church history focuses on the evolving story of men and women who struggle to live well with God and with one another. Three questions are woven throughout the biblical narrative: who is God, what expectations does God hold for humanity, and how have we fared in living with these divine intentions? Since there seems to be more than one God revealed in scripture, our responses to these questions depend upon whatever image we emphasize: some of us tend toward the Creator God, others God's mighty acts, still others divine majesty and omnipotence. For me, God's entering into covenant with a chosen people is key. Covenant thinking is central for those of us who wish to be addressed by God and respond to God's presence in our lives.

Where does the covenant come from? The prayer book catechism describes a covenant as "a relationship initiated by God, to which the body of people responds in faith" (BCP 846). One of the earliest is the Creator's universal covenant with Noah, his descendants, every living creature, and the earth (Genesis 9:1-17). In this account God's sign of faithfulness is a "bow in the clouds," which our ancestors colorfully imagined as a rainbow. It is followed by God's covenant with Abraham and Sarah, who are promised a multitude of descendants in return for their faithfulness, and God's covenant in Jerusalem with David and his royal line. Best known of all is the covenant with Moses on Mount Sinai, when God gives to him the tablets of the Law and says, "If you obey my voice and keep my covenant, you shall be my treasured possession out of all the peoples. Indeed, the whole earth is mine, but you shall be for me a priestly kingdom and a holy nation" (Exodus 19:5-6a). The conditional "if" is important because it implies a treaty between the strong and the weak: God's blessing and protection depend on the obedience and cooperation of the children of Israel.

It was not until the time of the exile that Israel saw a radically new kind of covenant, written not on stone, but on the heart. Jeremiah, the sixth-century prophet of the exile, wrote of it:

The days are surely coming, says the LORD, when I will make a new covenant with the house of Israel and the house of Judah. It will not be like the covenant that I made with their ancestors when I took them by the hand to bring them out of the land of Egypt—a covenant that they broke. . . . But this is the covenant that I will make with the house of Israel after those days, says the LORD: I will put my law within them, and I will write it on their hearts; and I will be their God, and they shall be my people. (Jeremiah 31:31-33)

The prophet speaks of a living relationship marked by the assurance of God's uncompromising faithfulness. This is no pie-in-the-sky promise. Jeremiah was writing at a time of brokenness when there seemed to be no ground for hope. It is precisely at such a time that God proclaims, "I will be their God, and they shall be my people." The biblical word used in the Hebrew Bible to describe the foundation of covenantal living is *hesed.* It conveys the loyalty and gracious loving-kindness of God. God's *hesed* is not an attitude or a legal arrangement; rather, it is a quality demonstrated in an active relationship with those who are vulnerable, particularly the weak, the needy, and the dependent.

Why is the covenant such an important touchstone for us today? It calls upon us, like our biblical ancestors, to mature and grow in our relationship to God and to one another. The people of God are called into a mutual relationship of faithfulness, chosen by God to live out love as justice-in-action. Jeremiah's "new covenant," written on the heart, carries ethical implications. It is echoed in the prophet Micah's proclamation of what is required of God's covenant partners: "to do justice, and to love kindness, and to walk humbly with your God" (6:8). In this text God's *hesed* becomes the expectation for our daily living. The covenantal promises we make in baptism include the promise to build up a faithful community. As biblical people called into a covenant with God, we are pointed toward faithfulness in action, toward loyalty expressed in loving relationships, and toward knowing God anew in the world. This biblical heritage signals fundamental change in our way of standing before God.

∿ 2. The Incarnation

The prologue to John's gospel speaks of the Word who "became flesh and lived among us" (John 1:14), the One who, in the words of the Nicene Creed, "became incarnate from the Virgin Mary" (BCP 327). The Incarnation is a promise that in Jesus God is with us in a new way. This doctrine affirms Jesus as fully God *and* fully human. There are other religious faiths that speak of gods who walk on earth and make transitory appearances in human form, as well as traditions that hallow those who speak with divine authority, much like the prophets of the Hebrew Bible. Yet the doctrine of the Incarnation is distinct: the Latin, *incarnatio*, actually means "being in flesh," a God who risks, suffers, and forgives. It extends beyond the birth of the Savior to include the deeds, teachings, death, and resurrection of Jesus. How this doctrine took shape in the councils and creeds of the early church is a story detailed elsewhere in this teaching series. The importance of naming the Incarnation here as one of the chief touchstones in Christian history lies in its proclamation of a God dwelling among us, who not only creates but also restores the dignity of human nature. That has far-reaching implications for us in all areas of our lives: in childhood and old age, in our work and achievements, in our efforts at connection and intimacy.[1]

In Anglican theology the legacy of the Incarnation is a cherished focal point. The Incarnation has become a guiding principle shaping Anglican understandings of humanity, the sacraments, and the material world because it underscores the potential goodness of humanity. While we traditionally acknowledge, as in the creeds, what the Incarnation says about who Christ is, we may overlook what it suggests about human capacities. Michael Ramsey, whom many of us remember as one of the great Archbishops of Canterbury of the twentieth century, concludes that "the Incarnation meant not only that God took human flesh, but that human nature was raised up to share in the life of God."[2] Richard Hooker, theologian and interpreter of the English Reformation, would have concurred: God took on the flesh of humanity to "change it, to better the quality" of human nature.[3] For South African Archbishop Desmond Tutu, incarnational theology means that the living Word of God is addressed to *all* people: through the Incarnation *all* men and women are moved closer to conformity with God's purpose and nature. In stressing God's initiative in moving toward us, the Incarnation provides a foundation for Anglican optimism about humankind.

Today Episcopalians express this optimism each time we commit ourselves in the Baptismal Covenant to "respect the dignity of every human being" (BCP 305). Even though pride and evil among humans and institutions must not be underestimated, an incarnational theology corrects our tendency to dwell only upon human unworthiness. Elizabeth O'Conner, who works with elderly poor women in Washington, D. C., writes:

> The journey we make into ourselves is not in order that we think poorly of ourselves, be made humble and dependent, but in order that we touch our divinity—know first hand that superior essence that dwells in us. You and I are called to vast things. We must ma-

ture, become ripe and full inside for our own sake, and for the sake of each other, and for God's sake.[4]

For me, one of the most important facets of the Incarnation is the theological base it provides for teaching about the sacraments—another linchpin of Anglicanism. We learn from Richard Hooker that the interdependence of divine and human natures we see in the Incarnation is the model for the "mutual participation" among Christ, the church, and humanity evident in the sacraments. A gracious spirit of mutual intent occurs, Hooker suggests, when human and divine will cooperate in offering eucharistic prayers. By virtue of the Incarnation Christ partakes of human nature, and by virtue of our eucharistic prayers we partake of Christ. This mutuality is directly expressed in our petition that as we offer to God "our selves, our souls and bodies, to be a reasonable, holy, and living sacrifice," so Christ "may dwell in us and we in him" (BCP 336). The purpose of Holy Communion, Hooker wrote, is changing human lives, not bread. At the end of the nineteenth century, theologian Charles Gore stressed the restorative social character of sacramental living.[5] At the conclusion of the eucharistic service, when the congregation asks God to "send us out to do the work you have given us to do" (BCP 366), we offer ourselves as willing participants in the ongoing drama of incarnation. The sacraments express our hope for bringing God to life in the world.

~ 3. The Gift of Baptism

Like covenant and incarnation, baptism is a gift initiated by God. It is also a form of covenant: through baptism new converts are recognized, welcomed, and forgiven of their sins. These new believers are born anew in Christ and dispersed, as at Pentecost, to be God's people at work in the world (see Acts 2). It is not the end of something, but the beginning of new life in Christ. As Paul's letter to Titus describes:

> When the goodness and loving kindness of God our Savior appeared, he saved us, not because of any works of righteousness that we had done, but according to his mercy, through the water of rebirth and renewal by the Holy Spirit. This Spirit he poured out on us richly through Jesus Christ our Savior, so that, having been justified by his grace, we might become heirs according to the hope of eternal life. (Titus 3:4-7)

Paul envisioned baptism as overcoming all that alienates and separates human beings from one another and God. It signifies God's promise of freedom and unity in Christ:

> As many of you as were baptized into Christ have clothed yourselves with Christ. There is no longer Jew or Greek, there is now no longer slave or free, there is no longer male and female; for all of you are one in Christ Jesus. (Galatians 3:27-28)

Baptism is *the* sign of Christian identity, which sets aside all prior identities. Although interpretations and practices of baptism varied in early Christian communities, it is clear that through baptism the young religious movement was growing into an expansive missionary body. Baptism, now as then, builds up the community of the church as the body of Christ.

Today Anglican liturgies have revived the biblical idea of baptism as a celebration whereby new members are recognized and welcomed. Baptism is, in general Anglican practice, the sacrament of initiation into the eucharistic community. It is the primary sacrament for each and every Christian. All subsequently evolving forms of ministry are grounded in baptism's lavish sacramental promises. Baptism promises, in the words of the catechism, "birth into God's family the Church" (BCP 858). Baptism extends our commitment to other family members. In the same passage in which John Donne reminds us that "no man is an island," he describes the church's action in baptism:

> When [the church] baptizes a child, that action concerns me; for that child is thereby connected to that body which is my head too, and ingrafted into that body whereof I am a member.[6]

Thomas Cranmer shaped early prayer book baptismal rites by often repeating the words "receive" and "promise": whether as infant or adult, we are all held in Christ's sacramental embrace. Those commitments and promises we offer in return—whether at our baptism or at our reaffirmation of the Baptismal Covenant—are responses to God's promise of forgiveness of sin. Baptized membership in the social community of the church grounds our commitment to God and to one another.

Baptism is my third touchstone particularly because of its emphasis on the themes that are important to me: Christian maturity and Christian learning. Accepting the promises of baptism underscores a willingness to be taught, to continue to be learners, to follow in the "apostles' teaching." Theologian Stephen Sykes describes baptism as the "framework for the whole of Christian living." No one, he adds, ever moves "beyond" it.[7] The phrase that Thomas Cranmer used in the early prayer books to describe this lifelong commitment was that baptism is "our profession." William Law, a popular eighteenth-century spiritual writer, echoes this intent: "Christians are by their Baptism...made Professors of Holiness." I wonder how many of us would readily describe ourselves as "Professors of Holiness"? Not many, I suspect. It might be helpful instead to think of this "profession" of Christ as a collective social and educational responsibility. Engaging with others in ongoing Christian education is one helpful response, for in truth most of us have more, not fewer, questions as we mature.

Baptism is also important to me because of its sense of hospitality: it creates an ever-expanding community. Nineteenth-century theologian Frederick Denison Maurice, who understood well the radical social dimensions of Christianity, taught that God's loving redemption was intended for all, including those of other faiths and religions. Responding to the hardening divisions among Christians of his day, he wrote: "It seemed to me that except I would address all kinds of people as members of Christ and children of God, I could not address them at all."[8] What Maurice had in mind was envisioning others clothed with the redemption intended by God. He taught that new life and understanding comes by living in the light of Christ's redemptive action, and not by dwelling on human sinfulness. In our own day Maurice's theological tolerance and open-mindedness are a model for our conversations with those of other faiths, as well as within our own church family. His stance is reminiscent of Paul's promise of baptismal unity in Galatians, a unity that overcomes classifications of sex, social status, race, and culture. Emphasis upon inclusive membership in the church is not a newfangled, contemporary idea. Anglicans can turn to Cranmer, Hooker, and Maurice, as well as to biblical foundations of baptism, to ground us as an expansive and welcoming body.

∾ 4. Bibles in English

This milestone is an obvious one for a historian of the Reformation like myself, since it is first and foremost a Reformation achievement: within a single century, access to

Bibles printed in the languages of the people transformed English and European Christianity. Today, at a time when most North American homes have three Bibles or more, we take for granted ready access to the Bible for private reading and corporate worship.

During the Reformation, technological and scholarly advances made the mass production of Bibles possible. The reformers built upon the scholarly legacies of the Renaissance, with its revival in knowledge of ancient and classical languages, including Hebrew and Greek. They desired to come as close as possible to the original texts; from the vantage point of the sixteenth century, the standard Latin translation of the Bible was deeply flawed. In the fifth century St. Jerome had originally prepared the Vulgate to meet popular demand for a Latin text, but by the eve of the Reformation Latin was no longer the language of the people, although it remained the language of the church. Moreover, in the thousand years since Jerome's translation, the medieval text of the Vulgate had accumulated the errors of generations of copyists and no longer met the high Renaissance standards for accuracy of translation and persuasiveness of rhetoric.

William Tyndale was the Reformation scholar who seized this opportunity to translate the Bible into English and return it to the people in a language they could understand. Printed in whole or in parts—a separate psalter, for example—the Bible was translated into the vernacular, everyday languages of Europe and England. We actually have Tyndale, and not King James, to thank for giving us the English Bible. His translations from the original Greek and Hebrew languages into English make up nine-tenths of the New Testament and most of the first half of the Old Testament in use in today.[9] Eighty percent of his language was included in the Authorized (King James) Version of 1611.

What stands out most about Tyndale's translation is its beauty: his unsurpassed ability with the sounds and rhythms of English resulted in poetic and memorable texts, a new kind of biblical prose. It was Tyndale who translated from the Hebrew the now familiar line in the opening chapter of Genesis: "Then God said, 'Let there be light'; and there was light." This replaced a Latin text which had read in English, "be made light and made is light." A contemporary example of our debt to Tyndale can be seen by contrasting Tyndale's Greek-into-English version of Jesus' words in John's gospel, "Let not your hearts be troubled," with a modern version, "Be not worried or upset." I don't know about you, but I prefer Tyndale! Because translating the Bible was politically dangerous at the time, Tyndale's insistence that biblical texts should be available to all eventually cost him his life. Yet the gift of his translations was passed on to others, and we are still recipients of that gift today.

In England reformers like Thomas Cromwell and Thomas Cranmer eventually authorized the sale of English Bibles, with texts that were largely based on Tyndale's translations. By the mid-1530s legal sanctions made it compulsory for English Bibles to be placed in every parish. So valuable and sought after were these Bibles that, like manuscripts in Tudor libraries, they were often chained to the lectern or reading station. In his preface to the 1540 English Bible, Thomas Cranmer observed that "the apostles and prophets wrote" in ways that might be understood by "every reader...for the amendment of life." Worshipers who use the prayer book today are familiar with a revised version of Cranmer's collect on scripture:

> Blessed Lord, who caused all holy Scriptures to be written for our learning: Grant us so to hear them, read, mark, learn, and inwardly digest them, that we may

embrace and ever hold fast the blessed hope of everlasting life. (BCP 236)

In effect the Reformation made this learning from scripture possible. The Bible was returned to the people as the handbook for Christian living. The ability of Christians everywhere to gain at least an elementary working knowledge of the Bible, the root of Christian faith, is a central Reformation achievement. With new translations of the Bible continuing to be printed today in the many languages of the world and throughout the global Anglican Communion, the tradition of the direct experience of hearing and reading the Bible remains fundamental.

～ 5. Common Prayer

My fifth touchstone is the idea of truly *common* prayer, another major legacy of the English Reformation. Just as we expect easy access to the Bible in English, we usually take the prayer book tradition for granted as well. I remember attending a Baptist funeral service as a young teenager. Although I found a Bible in the pew, I remember asking my friend where the prayer books were! My assumption was that every church would have such convenient books readily at hand. I had stumbled over the truth that I was a child of the Reformation, of biblically- and liturgically-based churches that grew and thrived following Gutenberg's mid-fifteenth-century invention of printing.

The language of late medieval worship in England and elsewhere was Latin. Religious services drew upon many liturgical manuscripts and texts, some with quite elaborate instructions for each commemoration. An unintended legacy of this pattern was that in time clergy came to have a monopoly over the liturgy, with the rest of the worshipers becoming more like spectators. When Archbishop Thomas

Cranmer prepared the first prayer book in 1549, a single innovative text replaced multiple service manuals and diverse medieval Catholic usages. The Reformation prayer book tradition is not only about ordering worship around one shared book. It is also about making common prayer easily accessible for all. For learned and unlearned, laity and clergy alike, the services in the prayer book were generally simplified and presented in a more manageable format, and invited communal responses.

Cranmer and the other reformers desired full participation in common prayer. All official church services were conducted in English, not Latin. One prayer book was provided for the public use of clergy and laity, a book that printed both the prayers and instructions for their use (which are called rubrics) for all to see. These and other changes meant that "liturgy" could once more become true to its original meaning as "the work of the people." In our own day a widespread movement for contemporary liturgical renewal in the Anglican Communion and other churches has continued to expand this tradition. Laity increasingly join clergy in the planning, preparation, and conduct of worship, with the expectation that all will join in common prayer.

Convenience in public worship was not the only intent of the prayer book. A specific theological legacy, emphasizing the sacramental value of the prayers of all the people, was embodied in the early prayer books. This focus can be found at the heart of reformed celebrations of the Lord's Supper: Cranmer turned the theological emphasis away from sacrificial actions performed by members of a sacred priesthood toward a wider perspective. He believed that in Holy Communion the church itself, and not just its ordained clergy, participated in the offering of the bread and wine. In effect he reclaimed a first millennium teaching from the *Liber Pontificalis* (the "Papal Book") that "every age concelebrates, young and old alike." While different roles remained for clergy and laity, the overall intent was that Holy Communion be a truly communal action. Later in his life Cranmer offered this explanation: "The priest and the ministers prepare the Lord's Supper, read the Gospel, and rehearse Christ's words, but all the people say thereto, Amen."[10]

This emphasis on full participation in common prayer may not seem as striking as other touchstones I have mentioned, but it brought about two liturgical changes that are especially important to me. First of all, it meant that the laity (and not just the clergy) received both the consecrated bread *and* the wine. The reformers wished to restore ancient biblical practice and encourage participation by all those present. So new was this practice of the laity receiving "communion in both kinds" (as it is formally called) that, when the English reformers returned the chalice to the people, a 1549 prayer book rubric instructed that the people "should drink once and no more." The people soon caught on: this rubric did not need to be repeated in the 1552 prayer book!

The other important change for me is Cranmer's decision to place the collect for purity near the start of the public service, where it remains today. The "Order for the Administration of the Lord's Supper" begins with these words:

> Almighty God, unto whom all hearts be open, all desires known, and from whom no secrets are hid: Cleanse the thoughts of our hearts by the inspiration of thy Holy Spirit, that we may perfectly love thee, and worthily magnify thy holy name; through Christ our Lord.

This is one of my favorite prayers and I cannot imagine beginning a traditional service of Holy Communion without it. Yet in pre-Reformation Catholic services, this collect was prayed in private and heard only by the clerics vesting for mass. With Cranmer's liturgical crafting it became part of the opening of the public eucharistic celebration. It is clear from the beginning of the new prayer book service that with all hearts open and all desires known, *all* of those present are invited to "perfectly love thee, and worthily magnify thy holy name." The central Reformation principle—which transformed English and European Christianity in the sixteenth century and still enlivens peoples from many continents—is that faithful living takes shape within communities where *all* members, and not just a few leaders, struggle to understand and live out the faith.

∾ 6. The Voice and Vote of Laity

The tradition of holding councils and other meetings for decision-making goes back to the second century, perhaps as early as the church council in Jerusalem recorded in Acts 15, when the "apostles and elders, with the consent of the whole church," discussed and agreed upon the admission of Gentile believers into the church. Those we would now call "laity" were certainly involved in making this significant decision. When Cyprian was elected bishop of Carthage in the middle of the third century, the populace—including laity, overseers, and presbyters—participated. However, by the end of the fourth century, the early church moved toward centralization and a new emphasis on clerical authority. Soon there were separate structures, with most decision-making delegated to ordained leadership. On the eve of the Reformation only a few reformers criticized this clerical domination, and fewer still would have recalled the original biblical and early Christian tradition of leadership exercised by the people of God. Once the Bible began to be more widely read, other patterns of church organization, or polity, began to be observed and debated. However, although Cranmer referred to the need to include lay participation at the diocesan level, the monarchy in England had no wish to set up synods or councils where laity could participate with full voice and vote.

The historic turning point in sanctioning lay leadership instead comes to us from the history of the Episcopal Church in the United States. The policy of the new American church was directly influenced by the egalitarian principles of the eighteenth-century Enlightenment. It reflected more democratic forms of representation modeled in the new government's Constitution. Accordingly, the Episcopal Church, in its first informal Convention in 1784, declared that "to make canons there be no other authority than a representative body of clergy and laity conjointly."[11] The first representative body was comprised of clergy and lay deputies, with the involvement of bishops added a few years later. The character of representative bicameral gatherings with two deliberating Houses, the House of Clerical and Lay Deputies and the House of Bishops, was confirmed by the 1789 Constitution of the new Episcopal Church. Since our constitutional beginnings in the United States, lay persons have played a prominent part in church polity, taking our place, as today's catechism notes, "in the life, worship and governance of the Church" (BCP 855). Canadian schemes for church governance early on also made lay participation obligatory.

The serious inclusion of laity in church synods—ours are called diocesan conventions, provincial meetings, and General Conventions—has continued as other Anglican churches have come into existence in New Zealand, Australia, and elsewhere. However, it was not until the 1880s that the Church of England first agreed upon establishing a House of Laymen, with later progress toward a General Synod and a House of Laity, established in 1969. My experience in working with international Anglican bodies is that some bishops are still surprised to find that laity in North American Anglican churches have real and not token authority. When challenged, I say that in North America we have recovered the spirit of Acts 15 by assembling a widespread leadership of the people of God. For lay people, this *is* tradition, a renewed emphasis on the responsibility of local churches to shape their mission and live their faith.

~ 7. Women in Mission

"I must be up and doing!" was the favorite saying of my maternal grandmother, who was also a proud descendant of the popular revivalist Dwight Lyman Moody. My grandmother's evangelical "old-time religion" was grounded in the domestic piety of her home, yet forcefully aimed toward the community and the world. At the start of the twentieth century, she belonged to a church that was actively involved in the local community and responsive to social needs as she and her sisters, cousins, and aunts perceived them. Living out her baptismal role, this woman was often the first to be at work in her community in good times and bad, simply doing "what had to be done" for all sorts and conditions.

Episcopal women today may not find the ministries of their mothers or grandmothers fulfilling, yet the active callings of their late nineteenth-century forebears stand as eloquent testimony to their passion for mission, renewal, and reform. In postbellum America (after the Civil War) the interests, reform activities, and institutional organizing of Episcopal women eventually transformed the Episcopal Church. It seems incredible to me to remember that my beloved great-grandmother and my grandmothers, three women who were seldom silent, were effective religious leaders at a time when American women were forbidden to vote in civic elections, much less in the church.

The character of parish outreach was largely shaped in the years from 1865 to 1914, from the end of the Civil War to the start of the "Great War." In this period church schools for children, Bible study classes for adults, voluntary support for missionary efforts at home and abroad, involvement in neighborhood social service activities, and networking among women in the diocese were all aspects of the church's growth. In 1860, at the start of Lincoln's presidency, one in seven Americans were church members; by the end of the century, over half of the population was affiliated with a church. Credit for this achievement in the Episcopal Church goes not only to outstanding missionary bishops like Jackson Kemper and James Lloyd Breck, who journeyed to the frontiers of the midwest, but also to legions of churchwomen, who were often the effective instigators of new parishes.

Anna Julia Cooper, a noted African-American educator and reformer, once called these women the most "potent...missionary agents" in the church. One extraordinary family, the Emery sisters, deserves credit for organizing Episcopal women's missionary efforts into the church-wide network first called the Woman's Auxiliary and today known as the ECW, or Episcopal Church Women. Both Julia Emery and her sister Mary Emery Twing worked to organize diverse women's groups into a national body, the Woman's Auxiliary of the Episcopal Church's Board of Missions, of which Julia Emery served as secretary for forty years. Eventually five general areas of missionary "usefulness" were defined for the Auxiliary: in the language of those days, the foreign, domestic, diocesan, colored, and Indian fields. Two other sisters, Susan and Theresa Emery, wrote for a children's publication on mission and coordinated the sending of boxes of supplies out to Episcopal missionaries in the field, fifty percent of whom were women supported in their work by women philanthropists through the United Thank Offering (UTO).

Yet the history of these women is by and large a hidden history. Because they were not professional theologians, church officials, or salaried employees of the church, the historic contributions of women like the Emerys remained invisible. The selectivity of the historian did not work in their favor; for a long time no one knew to look for them or to ask where they were. Historian Mary Sudman Donovan, among others, has labored to redress the balance and to give us their history. She argues, for example, that the tireless reform and charitable activities of women in the late nineteenth century preceded and created an openness to the "social gospel" before male theologians began to preach it in their churches:

> The labor force that implemented the social gospel—providing health care, education, and economic assistance to the disabled and the disadvantaged—was composed overwhelmingly of women. And the reason the Church was able to offer so many programs to ameliorate social evils was that churchwomen were willing to work for long periods of time either as volunteers or at extremely low wages. The women accomplished the social gospel with their actions, not their words.[12]

While churchmen from the 1860s onward discussed social problems, Episcopal women were among the first to organize charitable expressions of the social gospel. Their legacy is not one we should overlook.

∾ 8. The Civil Rights Movement

Few of us who came of age in the United States during the 1950s and 1960s will forget the challenges and tragedies of this period that ended with the assassinations of John F. Kennedy, Martin Luther King, Jr., and Robert Kennedy. For many in my generation these were years of activism, marches, "sit-ins" for civil rights, and rallies for peace and justice. I grew closer to my local church during those years, especially to the clergy and lay leaders involved in civil rights. The reason I have chosen this part of the civil rights era as one of my touchstones is that it proved to be a turning point in the Christian churches' advocacy of racial justice. During this time churches—including the Episcopal Church—were repeatedly and directly challenged to change their persistent habit of officially ignoring racial injustice.

Historical beginnings are hard to pinpoint exactly. Was the starting point of the modern civil rights movement the Supreme Court's unanimous ruling in 1954 on the unconstitutionality of racial segregation in the public schools? Or was the catalyst Rosa Parks's refusal in 1955 to move to the back of the bus, which inspired Martin Luther King's year-long bus boycott in Montgomery, Alabama? By the early 1960s the blunt question before us, as stated in the prayer book collect for social justice, was whether we as individuals and as a religious community would "contend against evil" and "make no peace with oppression" (BCP 260).

Each of us who lived through the moral challenges, turbulence, and violence of those years will have different specific memories. My own memories were shaped by an interracial action group named ESCRU, the Episcopal Society for Cultural and Racial Unity, founded in 1959. An ESCRU chapter was active in my hometown of Detroit, a city with a long history of racial tension. ESCRU's activist efforts to confront the reality of racism were apparent at the 1961 Detroit General Convention, when members of a prayer pilgrimage returned from "freedom rides" challenging segregated church institutions in the south and north. As the war against racial injustice continued and intensified throughout the decade, ESCRU members were among the thousands who marched with Martin Luther King, Jr., in Washington, D. C., and in Selma, Alabama. In those years I joined marches for civil rights while working at an interracial urban ministry site on the south side of Chicago. What had once seemed to me to be formidable barriers—between sanctuary and everyday society, and between peoples of different races and classes—eased as we labored together to advance civil rights.

I have focused on ESCRU, but others telling this story might rightly emphasize the history of prophetic witnesses among black leaders, parishes, and organizations within the Episcopal Church. For decades black Episcopalians waged a persistent struggle against what was, in effect, canonical apartheid in the church. A leader in this movement toward full civil rights was Alexander Crummell, the nineteenth-century African American who helped to found the Conference of Church Workers among Colored People, an organization that worked for racial justice in the church. The Conference for years provided educational and social leadership, and contended against efforts to segregate and disenfranchise black Episcopalians. It was the forerunner of the Union of Black Clergy and Laity, formed in 1968 and now called the Union of Black Episcopalians (UBE).

This period of history is a touchstone for me because I was personally involved in it, and through it was given a brief glimpse of what Paul meant when he told the Galatians of being "one in Christ." The civil rights era is part of

the "hidden" history of Anglicanism, when the predomi-
nantly white Episcopal Church broke out of a history of institutional denial and turned publicly to address racism.
Recent events and memories shape group identity as much
as historic achievements of long ago. The interracial activism in the 1960s left a prophetic legacy for Episcopalians
who continue to seek racial justice. As the Union of Black
Episcopalians' purpose statement accurately observes,
"The Church is not whole unless all of God's people are an
integral part of it."

～ 9. The Full Inclusion of Women in the Church

In naming the inclusion of women as one of my touchstones, I do not want to limit myself to women's ordination
to the priesthood, even though the ordinations in Philadelphia in July, 1974, and in Washington in 1975, and the actions of the Minneapolis General Convention in 1976 were
important turning points in the life of the Episcopal
Church. These events represented far-reaching changes in
theological understandings of ministry and leadership, but
to limit a consideration of the role of women in the church
to ordination is to miss out on the larger and still unwritten
history of the shifting attitudes toward women and leadership within the church.

At the start of the 1970s the question was still open:
would women and girls find their voices and gifts of service
fully welcomed in the church? It may be hard to imagine
today how vast and extensive the prohibitions were against
women and girls serving in a variety of parish roles thirty
and forty years ago. I told my nephew last year the story of
how his father, my twin brother, and I had tried and failed
to serve together as acolytes when we were his age. In the
same decade and parish, after years of faithful service as a
church school teacher, my mother was told that she could

not run for the vestry because "the social climate is not right." Being a lay reader was also controversial: permission for women to serve in this way was the result of a long, painful struggle to allow women to speak publicly in church. Even when women were allowed access to such roles, effective leadership was not always expected. For example, when I accepted in 1977 a professional position with the national church, I was told candidly, "I don't expect you to accomplish much as a woman; ask a bishop for help if you really want to get anything done"!

Imagine, for a moment, your parish without the public presence of lay women and girls in the service: no women as acolytes, lay readers, vestry leaders, ushers, chalice bearers. Of course, women were *always* there, quietly and sometimes invisibly "taking their places" on altar guilds, in church schools, as charitable donors, and in the kitchen. You might find it interesting to find out when women were first elected to the vestry in the parish where you worship, or when girls were first allowed to function as acolytes. What other changes have there been in local leadership patterns? My hunch is that you will find most changes involving the participation of women and girls occurred in the 1960s and 1970s, with some as late as the 1980s.

The story of women's struggle to serve as elected lay deputies in the House of Deputies is an instructive case in point. Efforts to elect women deputies took over fifty years. Opportunities were missed in 1919, when the General Convention defeated a plan to elect women to the Board of Missions, and again in 1946, when the diocese of Missouri brought Mrs. Randall Dyer as one of their regularly elected deputies to the Convention. When, after much debate, the male deputies offered to seat her without voice or vote, she declined this "courtesy." Efforts to elect women deputies continued through subsequent Conventions. In 1961 the

House of Deputies defeated by the largest margin ever another proposal for women deputies. In 1964, when Clifford Morehouse, president of the House of Deputies, once again proposed the election of women as deputies, he added: "The truth of the matter is that men and women are equally loyal communicants of the church and the practice of segregation by sex is no more admirable than that of segregation by race or color."[13] This was one of many times in the history of women's struggle for leadership when parallels were drawn with racial segregation. The decision to approve women deputies finally came at the 1967 General Convention and was ratified at the 1970 General Convention in Houston, when forty-three women were permitted to serve their church as full-fledged representatives and legislators. History was made in Houston. When those women deputies took their seats, the longest legislative battle for lay women's leadership in the Episcopal Church was over.

In the same General Convention, the full admission of women into the diaconate was officially approved, while at the same time ordination to the priesthood was denied. As deacons, women were acknowledged as clergy. Like their male counterparts, they were entitled to be called "The Reverend." In 1971 the Episcopal Women's Caucus was formed to "actualize the full participation" of women in the church, including ordination to the priesthood and episcopate, which was officially approved at the General Convention in 1976.

An image is worth a thousand words, or so the axiom goes. There, standing by the altar in 1989 at Barbara Harris's consecration as the first woman bishop in the Episcopal Church, was the diminutive, dignified, and graceful octogenarian Florence Li Tim-Oi, the first woman priest in the Anglican Communion. She had been ordained in 1944 in wartime Hong Kong by a bishop needing to ensure pastoral care for Chinese Anglicans living under Japanese occupation. When the bishop and Li Tim-Oi were both denounced for this pioneering act, she quietly stepped aside to avoid further embarrassment to her bishop. Thus it truly was a historic sight to see Li Tim-Oi, after years of obscurity, standing by Bishop Harris's side. The long journey to the full participation of women in all three orders of ministry, begun at the start of the twentieth century, had come full circle. Women's ordination in the Anglican Communion began in Hong Kong; it was not invented by the Episcopal Church.

The admission of women to all three orders of ministry is a touchstone that symbolizes a biblical truth: baptism is the foundation for all ministry. It also has the power to change and inform basic understandings of ministry among the laity, both women and men. The traditional biblical term *laos*, which is the Greek root of the word for "laity," once again includes all the priestly people of God, women as well as men, lay as well as ordained.

∼ 10. The Recovery of Spiritual Life

I have given a good bit of thought to whether I should include the newly emerging fascination with spirituality as a significant turning point in the church's history. Am I being too optimistic? It is impossible to know whether there truly are increasing numbers of contemporary believers, churchgoers or not, who are seeking to know the spiritual reality at work in their everyday lives over the long term. Yet I am inclined to see this movement as a turning point, with gifts and graces that will propel us faithfully into the new millennium.

While "spirituality" is a term of relatively recent coinage, lay mystics, poets, and theological visionaries—from

Julian of Norwich to Evelyn Underhill, from Benedict of
Nursia to T. S. Eliot, from Richard Hooker to Emily Dickinson—have for centuries inspired Christians to take spiritual journeys in this world. These and other authors of
spiritual "classics" emphasize both humanity's "immer-
sion in God" in this world and the people of God as corpo-
rately engaged and socially responsive.

I have two favorite definitions for "spirituality." The
simplest one comes from Joan Chittister, the contemporary
Benedictine writer who describes spirituality as "theology
walking." All that we think, feel, and say about God—that
is, all that comprises our theology—is expressed as we
daily walk about with our beliefs. Spirituality is theology
walking. The other comes from a much earlier Anglican
author of spiritual guidebooks, Jeremy Taylor, who observed how busy and full human lives are and how little
time there is to set aside for God. Does that sound familiar?
He encouraged his contemporaries to reimagine spirituality as encompassing everything a believer does. By direct-
ing all our actions to the glory of God, he wrote, our lives
become "a perpetual serving of God." Taylor reassuringly
adds, "We can no more be removed from the presence of
God, than from our own being."[14] Spirituality encompasses everything we do.

More and more Christians are finding that the church
building is not the only place to encounter and know the
holy. An innate sense of the spiritual character of all of life
seems to be increasing among today's believers. Upon reflection, I realize that this last of my ten touchstones also
embodies my hope for the future. It expresses a characteristic I have increasingly noticed in many Episcopal parishes.
There is growing interest in private prayer and meditation,
not as a substitute but as a companion to corporate worship, and the past two decades have seen a desire for pri-

mary texts of spirituality that is historically paralleled only by the sixteenth-century hunger for religious writings following the publication of English Bibles. Today's interest in deepening our spiritual journey is clearly a "rediscovery" built on the achievements of generations of monastics, holy women and men, and everyday spiritual seekers throughout the ages.

⟋ The Best of Pasts

This overview of my selected "touchstones" is, of course, too limited. The minute I wrote down the first ten items, others came to mind. What about the Sunday school movement and the rapid growth of Christian education from the mid-nineteenth to the mid-twentieth century? How could I forget continuing legacies of prayer book revision? The listing could continue. There are stories I have not passed on. A historian's work is never complete. Yet the ten themes I have selected provide good beginnings for extending knowledge of the past and expressing hope for the future.

In my rapid recounting of Christian history with a distinct Anglican and Episcopal emphasis, I have stressed people and events that others might not. My primary commitment, and my longstanding interest as a historian, has been to recover knowledge about ordinary Christians, clergy and lay. I want to understand better their contributions and achievements, both large and small, from the past and present. Many histories of the church are written as if bishops and popes were the only significant players. I have not intended to slight leading bishops and other well-known clergy, but their stories have been chronicled in other histories. On the other hand, I have read many parish and diocesan histories that proceed without mentioning laity, and accounts of church life that ignore women and youth, racial and ethnic groups. I have, in my listing, only begun to address these distortions. Meanwhile, I remain primarily eager to know more about Christians whose daily work lies in the world. There is important history here that we have not remembered. The history of how these Christians have reclaimed, shaped, and changed their understandings of ministry is a topic worth exploring at length in the following chapter.

Knowledge of history can also serve as a moral compass or guide. It is important to name and honor the struggles and achievements of ancestors in every generation who have labored for freedom and justice. A modern author has written, "The past can be more liberating than the future if you're willing to identify its evasions, its distortions, its lies, and unleash its secrets and its truths." We are not bound by the past. Rather, each time we critique and examine our history, it yields new information that can guide us toward more liberating futures. If we wish to have the "brightest of futures," we need to know the "best of pasts."[15]

Chapter Three

The Ministry
We Share

Afriend of mine, Elisabeth, is eighty years old and maintains a truly astounding schedule of visiting the "old people," as she calls them, of her parish. She loves listening and talking with them. Listening, really listening, is one of her special gifts. St. Paul would have called it her *charism*, a gift of God for building up the body of Christ in the world. Elisabeth recently told me that she decided to relish her own gift for ministry more by increasing the number and, as appropriate, the length of her visits. She made this decision in response to a sermon from a young woman priest about the "ministry we all share." "I finally caught on," Elisabeth said, "that the gift was within me all along. This ministry business is about being who we truly are."

"This ministry business is about being who we truly are." Elisabeth's response may not sound dramatic. Perhaps you had to know her to savor, as I did, her newfound delight and determination. Maybe you know people similar to Elisabeth, friends who are growing into their identity as Christians as well as exploring what ministry means in their lives. Elisabeth's understanding of ministry—that it is about affirming our God-given gifts and graces in daily living—is an insight that is catching on more and more in Episcopal parishes. Elisabeth is fortunate: the clergy and leaders of her parish envision ministry as an everyday gift promised in the Baptismal Covenant. Together members of this community sustain and nurture one another as they live into the biblical promise of relationship with God.

In the previous chapter we looked back over the history of the church and identified ten important touchstones that still influence who we are today. Among these I included covenant-making, baptism, and the inclusion of all the people of God in the leadership and decision-making of the church. These perspectives on laity are important to me as a historian because they remind us of things we already know and surprise us with new things. They are part of the "unwritten history" of the church, so often overlooked and unnoticed. Part of the historian's vocation is to seek out and discern what these unwritten histories are, in order to give the whole picture of our present and our past.

Verna Dozier, a teacher of the Bible who makes strong claims for the authority of the laity, advocates the importance of recovering this history and sees today's conversations about the ministry of all the baptized as a recent but hopeful improvement. "Back when I first started talking about ministry," she says, "it was something the ordained did." Expanding this vision of ministry has been a long, uphill struggle. The development of ministry for laity and clergy has varied from century to century and context to context. The history of laity in the life of the church has indeed been complex. Dozier argues that, along the way, the institutional church gradually co-opted the biblical sense of ministry as properly belonging to the whole people of God. For centuries, clear and compelling support for the ministries of lay persons in the world has been peripheral in official church structures even though, as Dozier notes:

the church is the people of God. It takes two forms, the
church gathered and the church scattered. We gather to
break bread as a community, to hear our story, and to
recommit ourselves to the dream of God. We scatter to
live into that dream. It is the task of the church, the people of God, to minister within the structures of society.
It is the role of the church, the institution, to support
that ministry.[1]

Thus the "gathered" church supports the central ministry
of God's people at work in the world. In fact, when we truly
honor the ministry of the people of God, we are recovering
an important biblical tradition. We have come a long way
in catching up with our earliest roots, reforming and renewing our understandings of Christian leadership and responsibility.

The ways we talk about ministry are shifting as well.
Most of us, for example, would be surprised to learn that
the terms "laity" and "clergy," as we use them today,
would have made little sense in early New Testament communities. Our biblical ancestors customarily envisioned
what we today call "ministry" as belonging to all believers.
In early Christian communities, "service"—one of the
words interpreted by Paul as "ministry"—was seen as an
essential component of life in the new creation. In early
Christianity, every person counted. All believers were
agents of God's reconciling love. In a deservedly famous
chapter from his first letter to the Corinthians, Paul praises
the wide diversity, flexibility, and fluidity of the gifts dispersed among the gathered community, gifts designed to
build up the body of Christ:

Now there are varieties of gifts, but the same Spirit; and
there are varieties of services, but the same Lord; and

there are varieties of activities, but it is the same God who activates all of them in everyone. To each is given the manifestation of the Spirit for the common good. (1 Corinthians 12:4-7)

This chapter from 1 Corinthians is a ringing endorsement of the singular and social nature of ministry as it was intended to function in the diverse communities of our biblical ancestors. Yet I must confess that as a child, I had a different understanding. I was quite sure who *the* minister was: the rector, of course. In the early 1950s, the decade that some have called the golden age of the Episcopal Church, I do not remember being taught that each of us had a ministry. Nor can I recall laity being affirmed as "ministers" in the 1928 *Book of Common Prayer,* the prayer book of my youth. In fact, I do not remember the terminology about "ministry" shifting significantly in vernacular use until the early 1970s. By then the national Episcopal Church had begun to sponsor workshops on "lay ministry." Such workshops pointed to the startling claim in the proposed new prayer book that "the ministers of the Church are *lay persons,* bishops, priests, and deacons" (BCP 855). The catechism further asserts that the church carries out its mission "through the ministry of all its members" (BCP 855). At first, a number of persons found this naming of laity as "ministers" off-putting. For some it was confusing, for others "too assertive," and for yet others it smacked of clericalization, of trying to make lay persons into unpaid clergy. I remember one troubling conversation with a layman who believed that the institutional church, through this new language, was only seeking additional lay volunteers to carry out tasks *within* church structures rather than helping laity with their ministry in the world. However, there were many others, both clergy and laity, who heartily welcomed this renewed emphasis on lay ministry.

Today challenging questions still remain about the term "lay ministry" and its eventual effectiveness. Will "ministry" come to be acknowledged as extending into the world in theory *and* in practice? In practice, will "ministers" be seen as ordinary Christians living out their faith in society at large? Will theological and rhetorical consensus among professional theologians and ordained leaders about encouraging laity to exercise their vocations be accepted and enfleshed from the ground up? Can the linguistic and empirical gaps between clergy and laity, sacred and secular, be narrowed by envisioning ministry as a mutual enterprise, or by stressing, like Paul, our interdependence? Or will the modern western tendency to separate "sacred" from "secular" dimensions of life persist? What wisdom can we garner from the witness of biblical and early Christian ancestors about envisioning more holistic and less fragmented lives?

These questions are complex and interrelated. They are pertinent to the church's future as well as to its past. They are part and parcel of historical understandings about traditional patterns of ministry and leadership. In liturgical churches, these questions are also directly related to changing patterns of worship. When I was working with a parish Lenten study group on tradition and change, one frustrated member insisted that she loved "the old Father-Knows-Best days most of all." Among other things, she was bothered that there were so many lay persons up front, visibly "doing things" as part of the Sunday service. As we talked a bit more, she was surprised by my suggestion that such involvement was in tune with our biblical roots; it did not fit her understanding of the traditionally "right thing" to do in church. Her sense of surprise underscores the fact that the history of ministry is itself a story about changing traditions and assumptions in the church.

It is thus important to turn now in this chapter to the foundational biblical and early Christian understandings of ministry as the enterprise of the whole people of God. I wish to emphasize those whom Paul describes as "the body of Christ" at work in the world. I will pursue this conversation about the gradual reclamation of biblical emphasis on God's people by taking a look at some of the tricky language issues involved. Terms like "laity," "clergy," "priest" and "priesthood," "ministry," and "vocation" have a checkered past of changing usages. There are other terms like "*laos*" and "overseer" that are useful to know. Our operative definitions of "church" also significantly influence expectations about ministry. The current threefold pattern of ordered, or ordained, ministries—bishops, priests, and deacons—has changed and adapted to new circumstances. Reviewing these terms and briefly noting their historical development can help us shape a common language and basic framework for future conversations about ministry.

I also wish to illustrate the advantages of broad visions of ministry by focusing on the lives of four significant Anglican leaders, all lay people. Every history book should have its heroes and heroines, incarnate individuals and leaders whose lives offer inspiration. This book is no exception. While a number of candidates across the ages come to mind, I have chosen twentieth-century leaders. This century, after all, will soon be described in the past tense as part of history. The four Anglicans I have selected all share the gift of seeing God's reign broadly across a wide canvas. They have lived, or are living, what we today might call active lay ministries. The guides I have selected to assist in this panoramic view are Evelyn Underhill, William Stringfellow, Verna Dozier, and Charles Willie. These visionary

saints of God remind me in empowering ways that the
church is much larger than an institution. The lives and
wisdom of these lay leaders, authors, and activists illustrate ministry at work among the people of God. Incarnationally, they will help us define basic terminology about
ministry among the laity.

～ No Second-Class Citizens

What are some of the basic "ABCs" we can use in conversations about ministry? Biblical perspectives are essential, although we must be careful not to read our contemporary
assumptions directly into their ministerial contexts. Our
biblical ancestors would find it difficult to recognize their
linguistic patterns and assumptions about Christian leadership in our daily practices. As I mentioned earlier, our
Christian ancestors did not divide believers into two separate groups of clergy and laity, or even into priests and people. Much of the terminology about ministry which we
employ today in the institutional church has been influenced by post-biblical assumptions. In this section I want
to reexamine biblical foundations to recover some of the
central understandings about both ministry and the
church. This larger perspective is important. Our theology
of the church—that is, our *ecclesiology*—directly influences
our understandings of ministry.

Many terms and phrases are employed to represent the
church in scripture. The most frequently used language in
the Old Testament emphasizes that those called by God are
not just a people or *any* people. Rather, they are *God's* people. This call to be different is clear, for example, in this
message to Israel:

> For you are a people holy to the LORD your God; the LORD
> your God has chosen you out of all the peoples on earth

to be his people, his treasured possession. (Deuteronomy 7:6)

The assembly brought together by God's call is collectively named "the people of God." The New Testament also favors this term and adds language about God's people being "the body of Christ." In his chapter on spiritual gifts Paul tells the Corinthians, "Now you are the body of Christ and individually members of it" (1 Corinthians 12:27). These two phrases—"people of God" and "body of Christ"—are complementary. Together they represent those beloved of God.

This terminology employs the usual Greek word for people or "citizenry," which is *laos*. The extended biblical phrase for "the people of God" is *laos tou theou*. This term, typically shortened to *laos*, encompasses one reality. It does not distinguish between roles of ministry among the people, between laity and clergy. Rather, it designates a community united by a single call. When theologians refer to the church as "the people of God," the *laos*, they are typically referring to the whole community called forth in baptism, clergy and laity together. So the first biblical assumption worth emphasizing is that the church is God's people at work in the world. It is not an organization, or what we in modern centuries would call an institution; nor is the church in biblical terms a building. Such modern representations of the church would be far too small for our biblical ancestors.

Another assumption in the New Testament is that God's call to holiness is envisioned for all. Along with the other authors of the epistles, Paul makes it clear that a wide variety of different gifts and graces were at work in early Christian communities. In the twelfth chapter of 1 Corinthians we considered earlier, Paul explicitly underscores the concept of the faithful members of the body of Christ endowed

with different gifts of the Spirit, or *charisms,* freely distrib-
uted among them for the good of the whole. Modern scholars of Roman Catholic traditions have observed that the
notion that the most important gifts would be concen-
trated "on one man (even an apostle) or in a select group—is
one that Paul dismissed" with ridicule.[2] Our New Testament ancestors were reluctant to apply sacred terms to individuals.

This was not because scripture lacked references to religious officials. There were certainly priests in the Old Testament who served various gods. Anglican theologian
John A. T. Robinson once observed that one of the most
striking things about early Christianity was the lack of individuals permanently assigned cultic responsibilities for
mediating the holy. Instead, the whole people of God shared
in ordering, forming, and nurturing one another to be
God's people. Thus the author of 1 Peter speaks about the
priestly ministry embodied within the corporate whole:

> But you are a chosen race, a royal priesthood, a holy na-
> tion, God's own people, in order that you may proclaim
> the mighty acts of him who called you out of darkness
> into his marvelous light. Once you were not a people,
> but now you are God's people. (1 Peter 2:9-10a)

The letter uses powerful images to reassure a community
facing severe persecution. This courageously shared "royal
priesthood" conveys New Testament understandings about
all those who embody the holiness of God. The German reformer Martin Luther recovered this formative biblical tradition in the sixteenth century when he advocated the
"priesthood of all believers." Today liturgist Aidan Ka-
vanagh refers to the *laos,* "God's own people," as "a priestly
term" for priestly people. I think the New Testament

authors would have applauded this intent. God's call to holiness, priesthood in its general sense, is given to all.

The early Christian communities were formed through their Hebraic roots by a strong corporate, rather than individual, ethos. Members of these communities faced intermittent persecution, so belonging to such a body was not as simple as joining another volunteer association. These sisters and brothers were called into new life through their baptisms, and they experienced a broadly charismatic movement of the Spirit as they offered their gifts in service of the whole body. Here the original use of the term "charismatic" properly designates all believers, not one particular segment of the church. In social terms the baptisms of early Christians called forth their public identity and established community, as did their desire to continue passing on the apostolic tradition of the one they knew as Jesus of Nazareth. There were no second-class citizens in this household. All carried the religious authority of baptism, and all were agents in the central ministry of reconciliation. Thus a third biblical observation, one we also observed in the last chapter, is that the church is a community of people living in a covenantal relationship with God that is initiated and enacted in baptism. This ministry invites all members of the church, as the catechism states, "to carry on Christ's work of reconciliation in the world" (BCP 855).

～ Changing Patterns of Ministry

In early Christian practice, when members of a house church gathered to celebrate the eucharist, the one presiding was typically a prominent member of the family who was asked (as often happens today) to offer the blessing at a meal. In the days before Christian communities became more organized, even the elder assigned oversight for the whole, named as an "overseer" or a "bishop," held a rotating position. Amid such fluidity and diversity, "ministry" had various meanings. An early and common usage of the Greek term *diakonos* typically referred to an "assistant," or to any person assigned to a role in the liturgy. In the early centuries of the church's life those called "deacons" were typically persons "assisting" under the authority of an overseer or bishop. In the nineteenth century, a number of Protestant theologians in Germany began to emphasize that "ministry" meant "service" (in Greek *diakonia*). These religious leaders were interested in reviving the office of the deacon as a ministry devoted to acts of charity among the dispossessed. Their emphasis has now become common-place in the contemporary revival of the diaconate. It is rep-resented, for example, in the catechism's reference to the ministry of the deacon as a "servant of those in need" (BCP 856). It is common today to refer to deacons as represent-ing and expressing the "servant ministry" that belongs to the whole church. In some contemporary discussions, all of ministry is envisioned as "servanthood." This language is biblically apt in the general sense that, whatever form of Christian ministry we intend, we are offering service to God and God's reign.

In the early church, the use of language about clerical roles was much more fluid than that represented by the threefold ordained ministry named in today's prayer book. At most there are biblical hints, found toward the end of the New Testament era in the epistles to Timothy and Titus about duties that would, in later centuries, evolve into an established threefold pattern of ordained leadership: bish-ops, priests, and deacons. By the end of the third century, Christianity's original charismatic movement gradually became more organized, with specific officials assigned various responsibilities. For example, "priesthood," which we have generally described as the collective character of all members of the church, came to be named as the special province of elders called "presbyters" or "priests." The Latin term here is *sacerdos*. The "overseers" of the church—designated in Greek as *episkopos* and the ancestors of today's bishops—were originally called "presbyters" as well. These terms were used interchangeably. Over time, bishops became the unchallenged heads of colleges of presbyters, while presbyters (priests) emerged as those specifically delegated to preside at eucharists in the absence of the bishop. In the third century there are also references to "laymen," who are described as those who received spiritual assistance from clerics and who provided the latter with financial assistance. What seems to have happened overall is that by the end of the fifth century the *laos tou theou*, the people of God, were beginning to be seen as two groups, "laity" and "clergy." This division led the church away from the fundamental biblical understanding of the *laos* as all the people of God. Meanwhile, distinct priestly, diaconal, and apostolic ministries were developing for ordained leaders.

Throughout the middle ages, roles and functional definitions within the church continued to change and adapt to meet new circumstances. Later epochs, particularly the twelfth century, reinforced other distinctions between clergy and laity in dress, education, marital status, and morality. In the Christian west, clergy were exempt from civil and military service and from civil courts and taxation; they were required to live a celibate life, and thus to remain unmarried. A theological shift also pervaded these changes in role expectations, as sacred and sacramental powers became increasingly identified with ordained persons. In effect, by virtue of their ordering, or ordination, clergy were seen as "set apart" in character from the people who received their sacramental actions. By the end of the middle ages, the emphasis was on "sacred priests" serving laity. According to Verna Dozier, the error on this "slippery road" of ministry development was not the natural desire to name specific functions. It was "assigning to one part the designation that belonged to the whole people of God—holiness."[3] In the medieval theology of ministry, clergy were sacramental persons whose role was to foster devotion and piety among the people. This was the ministerial landscape on the eve of the Reformation.

During the sixteenth century, reformers like Thomas Cranmer in England and Martin Luther in Germany endeavored to return to practices of ministry that were more in harmony with biblical images of the church. Their efforts did succeed in breaking down some of the unnecessary distinctions between clergy and laity in Europe: reformed clergy were permitted and even encouraged to marry, and most gave up their late medieval clerical privileges and assumed the ordinary responsibilities of citizenship. The general Reformation perspective on vocations was that all persons were called to faithful living, and all were invited to participate in the sacraments and common prayers of the church. In the English church, the basic understanding of ministry was not so much Luther's "priesthood of all believers" as a community of diverse Christian vocations bound together by common prayer.

It is important to remember too that these English reformers extended the general population's access to works of piety and devotion by providing English Bibles and English prayer books for use by all. The reformers also sought to renew biblical preaching as a regular practice in the church's life: the proclamation of the Word soon became a central component in the practice of ministry. Accordingly, the church was described in the English Articles of Religion (as well as by leading continental reformers) as the place "in which the pure Word of God is preached, and the Sacraments be duly ministered" (BCP 871). Two centuries later, in North America, emphasis on the word grew to the extent that a clergyman might popularly be called "the preacher."

∼ Recovering the Ministry of Laity

Although these innovations of the Reformation succeeded in removing some of the distinctions between clergy and laity that had accumulated during centuries of medieval Catholicism, others remain to this day. For example, efforts to support religious education for laity as well as for clergy were intermittent and ineffective. The practice of catechesis—the instructional formation of Christians that had been a significant element in the early church's preparation of candidates for baptism—had been abandoned in the middle ages and was not reinstated after the Reformation. With today's renewed emphasis on adult formation, some church leaders are working to revive catechumenal instruction as a way of strengthening religious formation for laity. Others are supporting adult education as an ongoing component of parish life.

Today another problem with recovering the biblical emphasis on the ministry of the whole people of God relates to the modernist tendency to divide human experience decisively into "sacred" and "secular" components. This distinction, prevalent in western cultures, is no older than the eighteenth-century Enlightenment. Whatever its cultural origins, such a division would not have made sense to our biblical and early Christian ancestors. They viewed God's creation as one grand and holy gift. The people of God, as the lives of our Hebrew and New Testament ancestors amply testify, worked out their salvation in the world. Members of medieval and Reformation churches shared these assumptions. Contemporary Christians have to guard against the temptation, bequeathed by the coming of modernity, to separate sacred concerns from secular affairs and to divorce faith in God from daily life, keeping religion in a separate private sphere and dividing our thinking, our language, and our lives in two. In such a fragmented world, it is no wonder that "lay ministry" might be considered an oxymoron, a conjunctive phrase that does not make sense. There are other reasons why language about "lay ministry" is problematic. In the church today there are some who continue to hold the medieval assumptions about the second-class vocations of lay people and the elevated sacred character of the ordained ministry. These assumptions are reflected in our language: in English usage the term "lay" carries second-class implications. Byron Rushing, a state legislator and longtime lay deputy to General Conventions from the diocese of Massachusetts, rightly asks, if we wanted a second medical opinion, would we go to a "lay doctor"? Or if we needed a lawyer to defend our best friend, would we seek out a "lay lawyer"? Then why would we go to a "lay minister" to learn more about God's presence in our lives? It may well be that the term "lay ministry" itself is redundant since ministry at its most essential and basic belongs to the whole community. Thus Byron Rushing prefers using the biblical term "saints" to represent all believers, just as Paul addressed his letter to the Romans to "all God's beloved in Rome, who are called to be saints" (1:7). Similarly Tom Ray, bishop of Northern Michigan, speaks of the priestly, diaconal, and apostolic ministries that belong to all baptized persons:

> Priestly ministry explores the ministry of reconciliation, inclusion and unity. Where does most priestly ministry occur? At home—in the kitchen, the bedroom, the family room. At the workplace among employees.

Diaconal serving originates whenever we seek peace and justice and respond to human need. Apostolic ministry explores, among other facets, cooperative oversight. What of the oversight of our environment, on the playground, in business, in our judicial system, or the awesome oversight of parenting?[4]

I admire this sensitivity to biblical and early Christian components of ministry. The only concept I would add is baptism. When we speak of "baptismal ministry," we are reminding ourselves that our high calling as people of God is embraced sacramentally and communally in baptism. The primary sacrament of ministry lies in the calling of the baptized, not in ordination.

One final example of our fuzzy thinking about ministry and faithful living is the notion that clergy have "vocations"—that is, direct callings from God—while laity, at best, have "jobs." This misguided assertion assumes that God "calls" (the Latin word here is *vocari*) only ordained leaders. The leading matriarchs and patriarchs of our tradition—from Abraham, Sarah, and Hagar to Moses, David, and Samuel, from Mary and Martha to the Samaritan woman at the well—would have been surprised at this news. I recently heard an Anglican bishop from overseas argue that women could not be ordained because this "was not directed in scripture," only to be gently reminded by a scholarly monk that "scripture does not explicitly direct that *anyone* be ordained." Instead, a central biblical assumption about vocation is that God's call is intended for all who will hear it. This probably does not mean that God has a specific job or function picked out for everyone. Nor does it mean that we need to wait for a single dramatic event when a "call" is revealed to us, although theatrical moments can often be a part of experiencing God's call and our response.

Instead, the biblical roots of vocation are simpler and more intimate. Bishop Rowan Williams identifies these roots in the close association of "calling" and "creating" in the Hebrew scriptures. God calls and creation springs forth in an answering response. This creation theme, established in Genesis, is repeated in the psalms when God determines the number of the stars and calls them each by name (Psalm 147:4). God calls us as a people and as individuals. Williams continues, "In the most basic sense of all, God's call is the call to *be*," that is, to be the persons we are created to be.[5] I used to think that my vocation was my paid employment, being a teacher; now I think that I have a gift, a *charism*, for teaching that I am fortunate enough to be able to express in my daily life and work. My vocation lies in my primary identity as a child of God. I try to live out my vocation, exercising whatever gifts I have been given, by being the person God created me to be. Artificially restricting terms like "vocation" to clergy is a misreading of the biblical tradition. Emphasizing what we *do* as the all-defining fact of our identity is a modern preoccupation that can keep us from knowing who God means us to *be*. Our basic belonging is to be the one *holy* people of God, laity and clergy alike, called by God to the everydayness of baptismal ministry.

My new friend Elisabeth was absolutely correct in her discovery that "this ministry business is about being who we *truly* are." When we think about our identity, when as Christians we "say who we are," it is important to remember our biblical inheritance. We are a beloved and treasured people, created and called by God, chosen as God's own in baptism, redeemed by Christ, and inspired with gifts of the Spirit to share in service and solidarity with others. We are sent into the world to be God's people in the here and now, to live into the new vision for human life that was articulated and lived out by a Nazarene carpenter, who was also rooted in an ancient understanding of God's call.

~ Seeing Differently, Seeing the Whole

"Poets and Christians... are people who believe in the power of words to effect change in the human heart," writes Kathleen Norris, herself a contemporary poet.[6] The power words have to "effect change in the human heart" is one of scripture's clearest messages. When I hear the Bible read aloud daily in Morning Prayer, I listen even to the most familiar passage as if I were hearing the story for the first time. My vision is expanded or clarified, and my heart is moved. Similarly, I am sometimes able to catch sight of a new vision, another insight, when I read the Bible on my own. I must confess, however, that I prefer reading and reflecting on scripture in the company of others, allowing their friendly perceptions to expand my sight. I have a good friend who is nicknamed "Bear" because she has a vast curiosity for seeing things broadly. Much like the bear in the children's story who climbs to the top of the mountain "to see what she could see," my friend enjoys viewing the vast expanse on the other side of the mountain.

I now would like to shift our vision from a broad overview of the history of various ministries in the church over time to a consideration of how baptismal ministry has been lived by members of the body of Christ in particular places and times. Let me briefly introduce the quartet of guides I have selected to help us explore this terrain. My first choice is Evelyn Underhill, who led many in the early years of this century to a deeper understanding of the spiritual life through her books, retreats, and work as a spiritual director. My second choice is William Stringfellow, a social activist, lawyer, and sharp critic of church and society in the middle decades of this century, and my third is Verna Dozier, a scholar of the Bible and exemplar of the changing role of laity in the church. My fourth guide is Charles Willie, a professor of education and urban studies, who is a skilled advocate for school desegregation and racial justice.

Does this list intrigue or surprise you? Once again, as in my naming of ten touchstones in Christian history, I have exercised the historical principles of selection and interpretation. I have chosen lay leaders whose theological biographies and daily living illustrate important perspectives on faithful living. Honoring these four saintly citizens suggests a full, rich history, since two of them are women, and two are African Americans—members of two of the populations in the church whose impact is often undervalued. Many more books are needed to recover the stories of lay persons from those races, classes, and cultures whose ministries and identities have been eclipsed, ignored, or trivialized. My assessment of the collective contributions that these four Anglicans have already made is intended as an illustration of the depth and breadth of the historical panorama of faithful living among the saints of God.

Each of these four leaders evoked larger images for faithful living in the world than those expressed by people who identify "the church" with "going to church." Perhaps this is because their allegiances and vocations were not sponsored by the institutional church. Nor did they hold (at least for long) official positions within church structures; rather, they were and are sharp-eyed and perceptive critics of the institutional church. Their reputations were sometimes made by books they authored or by the adult education lectures and speeches they gave, and by the decisions they made about where to invest their primary attention as agents of reform and reconciliation in the world.

Their biographies creatively enliven whatever definitional language we wish to use to describe ministry. These four leaders have, through their lives and faithful witness, effected change in human hearts. I value their assistance in helping us see the church more broadly as the people of God at work in the world.

Evelyn Underhill
Evelyn Underhill, who lived from 1875 to 1941, helped many in her generation see and know the spiritual reality of God's world. Her work is undergoing something of a revival these days, although her writing has never entirely been out of fashion. Her credentials are impressive: she wrote and edited thirty-nine books; twenty of them remain in print and new editions of her writings are regularly published. She was initially well-known as the author of *Mysticism*, a monumental, scholarly study published in 1911. In this volume she explains and advocates the virtues of this significant tradition in Christianity and other religions. In the early 1920s she turned toward focusing her life's work on spirituality and spiritual direction. She became known in her own day as a retreat director and author of devotional texts. As a woman she held several "firsts" in her society: the first woman to lecture in theology at Oxford (in 1921), and the first woman to offer retreats at Canterbury Cathedral. She befriended many great and small citizens of her own age, among them the poet T. S. Eliot and a young Michael Ramsey, who would later become Archbishop of Canterbury. Despite these and other marked achievements, Underhill's accomplishments have yet to be fully acclaimed. This is our loss. Many of her books deserve to be included among those frequently named as Christian "classics."

Her recent biographer and editor, Dana Greene, aptly argues that Underhill had a distinct advantage in seeing differently because she was a woman. As a woman living in a male-dominated church, she stood at the edge of religious and intellectual life. I believe she was also seen differently because she was a woman. One result is that some commentators have trivialized her interests, while others have interpreted her achievements in patronizing ways. I once heard her dismissively described by an American theologian as a good "theologian for women." Others have misinterpreted Underhill's insights as comfortable or "cozy." Far from it. Her definitions of spirituality are neither passive nor sentimental. They are bold. She deserves wider reading from women and men alike. Fortunately, contemporary interest in her area of expertise—spirituality—is reviving, and more of Underhill's books are becoming available. It would be a mistake, however, to think of Underhill as an early precursor of the "New Age" spirituality popular today in North America. She was not interested in seeking experiences of "the holy" as a consumer item, but instead was dedicated to the human possibility for recovering all senses of the sacred in our daily lives.

Her major contribution, as I understand it from reading many of her books, is her presentation of a religious reality that is accessible to all believers. Underhill envisioned the spiritual life as a "concrete fact...a real response to a real universe." She believed that the way we face reality was not complete without the richness and transformative insight of the spiritual life, and she incorporated insights from the new field of psychology into ways of enhancing spirituality. Culture, nature, memory, environment, unconscious and subconscious sensibilities, dreams and fantasies: all were transformative resources for seeking the fullness of God. Underhill served as a translator, framing the wisdom of those she called spiritual "pioneers" and mystics in terms that her contemporaries would understand. Traditional names for components of the spiritual life—the active, contemplative, ascetic, and apostolic—are presented by Underhill in the less formidable language of work, prayer, self-discipline, and social service. Many of her readers have found her clarity refreshing. Whether in her writings, radio addresses, or retreats, this articulator of the spiritual life stressed the opportunity we share for deepening our religious experience.[7]

Underhill was passionate about inviting all into the realization and pursuit of a spiritual life that was anchored in God. She believed our consciousness of being rooted in God could infuse all aspects of our lives. Her advice, as an author or spiritual director, is simple and direct. She encourages us to give the contemplative side of our nature a chance, letting "it breathe for at least a few moments of each day the spiritual atmosphere of faith, hope and love." Awe, reverence, imagination, and our powers of experiencing beauty and love are presented as dynamic opportunities for deepening our religious sensibilities and experiencing the fullness of our God-given humanity. Underhill does not advocate a passive spirituality, which she once decried as "armchair" mysticism and "comfortable piety." The kinds of naiveté and autonomous individualism that pervade some of today's religious self-help volumes have no place in her vocabulary. Her encompassing definitions of "spirituality" repeatedly stress practical, active contributions to the larger whole. In one of her most practical books, *The Life of the Spirit and the Life of Today*, she concludes, "Spirituality, as we have seen all along, must not be a lovely fluid notion or a merely self-regarding education; but an education for action." She repeatedly stressed the mystical tradition of returning to engage the world, and the mystic's desire for the betterment and greater solidarity of humanity. Action was imperative for Underhill. She pointedly insisted that the spiritual values of a society could never be fully realized as long as poverty prevailed. Working for structural change in society by relieving the systems of economic pressure that tormented so many was for Underhill a major component of the spiritual life.[8]

As a historian, I appreciate Underhill's enthusiasm for studying the lives of great saints and mystics. In describing the rich tradition of prayer, she pointed to many spiritual pioneers, including the founders of religious orders, such as Benedict of Nursia and Francis of Assisi; medieval mystics like Richard Rolle and Julian of Norwich; the evangelical revivalist and preacher John Wesley; and the prison reformer Elizabeth Fry. These were individuals who broke through the apathy and despair of their own societies to enliven the life of the Spirit. She warned against envisioning these heroic men and women as picturesque specimens from "spiritual epochs now closed," or nostalgically imagining them as "God's pet animals, living in an incense-laden atmosphere and less vividly human and various than ourselves." Instead, they are "constructive revolutionaries," much "like Christ Himself." In their lives of prayer, they recovered a "new use of antique tradition," which was itself rooted in direct contact with the Spirit. Being knowledgeable about the spiritual greatness of our ancestors, Underhill believed, deepens the vitality of knowing and loving God today. Underhill appreciatively describes the mysterious and energizing power of "spiritual personalities" to inspire prayer from generation to generation. She encourages us to enlarge our time-span by joining the "living spirit of the past" with the "living spirit in us."[9] I concur. I encourage students to engage history by putting ancient voices in conversation with modern ones.

Underhill saw broadly. Her scholarship about mysticism and her writings on spirituality and worship offered evidence of God's ongoing revelation. Her vision crossed and enlivened spiritual epochs. The church, for her, was more than creeds, dogma, and moral codes. The transforming personal experience of the love of God was more intimate and more expansive than any human institution could contain. Her way of seeing invited a richer, more traditional understanding of the spiritual life as widely accessible to the people of God. It is no wonder that Evelyn Underhill has been added to the church's calendar of lesser feasts and fasts. The collect commemorating her life underscores her value in teaching the church that we are "guided" by the "Spirit into the light of truth." If there is a twentieth-century Anglican founder of today's desire to live the spiritual life and know God's presence in everyday experience, she is Evelyn Underhill.

William Stringfellow

Born in 1928, Frank William Stringfellow had a passion for addressing the wrongs of the world. I first heard Stringfellow's name mentioned in the 1960s as a social activist lawyer who publicly supported disenfranchised miners, conscientious objectors, and other antiwar protesters. Then I began to read his writings. Many of his books have the incisive, searing character of a prophet's writings. Like Amos and Micah, he was passionately committed to the biblical message and to naming the destructive "principalities and powers" at work in his society. Stringfellow was a critic of church and society, and the fifteen books and countless articles he wrote were not bestsellers among institutional leaders, whether in the church or the state. I recall my local college rector advising me that Stringfellow's 1964 book, *The People is the Enemy*, was "too radical" to read. When I reread Stringfellow today, I regret among other things that I did not argue his merits more vigorously with those who dismissed his writings. Again I am reminded of Underhill's assessment that heroic pioneers of the faith are "seldom in harmony with [their] own epoch." Fortunately, like Underhill, Stringfellow's works are today enjoying a revival; a new accessible selection of his writings, *A Keeper of the Word*, is now available.[10]

Today, when popular statements about religion often seem shallow, I value Stringfellow's profound ability to speak the truth as he saw it. He was a champion of the biblical Word, as well as a fomenter of change in social institutions, including the church. Like Verna Dozier, he is best described as a "biblical theologian," one whose roots are deeply grounded in the living Word. He often wondered, when he was called a "lay theologian," if this was a way to trivialize his impact. I think that it is accurate and not dismissive to describe Stringfellow as a "popular theologian," an author who loved and learned from conversations about religion with friends, young persons, and people on the street. In his books, Stringfellow redefined for his contemporaries biblically-informed concepts of vocation, mature spirituality, and the church. In his life—whether as a pacifist, a lawyer working with the down-and-out, a provider of hospitality, or a challenger of institutional lethargy—he embodied the political cost of conscience on behalf of justice. He struggled daily with the challenge of living in modern times as a "biblical person" (a phrase he frequently used).

Our lives, Stringfellow insists, are inherently theological. We carry the incarnate good news of the gospel not as saints, but as human beings. He writes: "*We* are each one of us parables." I wonder if any of us would describe our life as "a parable"? Does this sound too dramatic or egocentric?

Yet Stringfellow is emphatic: our "vocation" is "being human, nothing more and nothing less." He describes vocation as being about the whole of life, about the here-and-now; it is "categorically" not about "being religious." This understanding of bearing the Word shaped Stringfellow's definition of mature spirituality. In his engaging 1967 book, *Count It All Joy*, he explains the delight of listening to the Word:

> When a person becomes that mature as a human being, one is freed to listen and at last to welcome the Word in the Bible, and one is enlightened to discern the same Word of God at work now in the world, in (of all places!) one's own existence as well as in (thank God!) all other life. Thus is established a rhythm in the Christian's life encompassing one's intimacy with the Word of God in the Bible and one's involvement with the same Word active in the world.

While Underhill reclaimed the classical tradition of mysticism as the transformer of contemporary spiritual life, Stringfellow's sense of the Spirit was saturated in the Word of God.[11]

His views of the church stress broad, collective movement. He describes the church as an "event" moving in time, a people not only carrying their religion with them but charged with responding to "the cares of the world." He emphasizes baptism as the authoritative and liberating foundation for this people's work in the world. He reads baptism biblically, focusing on the public and political promise in Galatians to overcome "all that alienates, segregates, divides and destroys human beings in their relationship with each other." Stringfellow was a forceful advocate of interdependence and reciprocity among all believers, once observing: "There is no priesthood without a laity serving in the world; there is no laity without a priesthood serving the laity." He wrote, if the church wishes to live up to its biblical mandate as a "Holy Nation," it cannot afford to overlook this "radical interdependence" among believers. Moreover, if the people of God want to be more than just "observers of religion," they must not confine themselves to the sanctuary or acquiesce into political silence. Stringfellow delighted in the promise made in the Baptismal Covenant "to respect the dignity of every human being." His reflections on ministry recall and reiterate this and other traditional biblical expectations.[12]

Stringfellow was a diligent witness to the biblical power of living what he called "the Gospel vocation." He emphasized characteristics of responsible Christian adulthood and, like Underhill, named practical resources for living the Word of God. First of all, he insisted that the ordinary person need not be a biblical scholar. Instead, listening and making oneself vulnerable to that Word are the essential requirements. He described attentive listening as the "most significant credential" for biblical interpretation. Stringfellow presented the "biblical lifestyle" as inherently "radical." Here again he has a biblical (rather than a narrowly political) connotation in mind, one that requires biblical persons to comprehend, confront, and transcend the powers of death at work in their lives. Stringfellow saw the church and the world as part of the continuing biblical drama where Christians, armed with the baptismal reverence for life, are called daily to witness to resurrection against the powers of death. As a street lawyer in Harlem, this biblical theologian would be described today as one who not only "talked the talk, but walked the walk." He left us the presence and power of his own witness, and a legacy of writings that can help Christians today recover a sense of being biblical persons at work in the world.[13]

Verna Dozier

Verna Dozier was a high school English teacher who in retirement has used her prophetic gifts nurtured in the black
church to speak of what she calls "the dream of God."
Dozier, like Stringfellow, is an unsparing critic of the institutional church. And, like Underhill, Dozier has been a
popular speaker and an influential workshop leader who
has appeared in person in most of the dioceses and many of
the parishes of the Episcopal Church. Her voice is com-
mandingly mellifluous, making us attentive to the Word
and her words. She carries the dignified authority of one
who was a teacher of English for thirty-two years in public
schools, a longtime lover of learning, literature, and poetry. She can read hymn texts out loud more musically
than many of us can sing them. Thus when Dozier proclaims "the mighty acts of God," it is as if we were there
too.

Similarly, her blunt observations about church and
ministry often have multiple dimensions. At first I think I
know what she means, then later on I find myself working
through the impact of her assertions and questions. Yes,
questions. Like most good adult educators, indeed like Jesus in the scriptures, Dozier encourages new understanding among her companions by asking questions. "Are you
content to worship Jesus?" she once asked a Bible study
group. At a conference on lay leadership she sent us away
with passages about David and Samuel in hand to reflect on
how our choice of a leader reflects our self-understanding.
It was thoughtful, demanding work. Her three books have
this quality as well. I find myself repeatedly unpacking and
unfolding her assumptions about ministry. Grasping the
implications of her assertions often leads me to look up and
linger over a compelling passage from scripture.

Three of Dozier's conclusions about ministry have also stayed with me over the years. I think the central impact of her work as a biblical theologian lies in leading us to embrace God's expansive dream for God's people, the church. Verna Dozier has done more than anyone else in the contemporary Episcopal Church to help its members—regardless of our roles and understandings about ministry—to think through what the church is meant to be. She envisions the church as a people with a biblical story and a dream to carry on. Somewhere early on in our post-biblical dreaming, she warns, the biblical images of the church were turned upside down, "and the Church, the people of God, became the Church, the institution."[14] Her recipe for reclaiming our biblical legacy includes familiar components—emphasis on community, baptism, creation, incarnation, and work to be done—yet she puts these ingredients together into a dream of God that is fresh, direct (if not blunt), and compelling:

> The urgent task for us in the closing years of this turbulent century is to reclaim our identity as the people of God and live into our high calling as the baptized community. We are a chosen people, chosen for God's high purposes, that the dream of God for a new creation may be realized. God has paid us the high compliment of calling us to be coworkers with our Creator, a compliment so awesome that we have fled from it and taken refuge in the church. God does not need such an institution.... The institution is replaceable. The living body of God's people is not.[15]

Unpacking the meaning and implications of this paragraph could occupy an adult study group for weeks. As with Underhill and Stringfellow, Dozier's passionate belief in the transforming power of God's love is clear. Envisioning a dream of God that is larger than the institutional church, she invites us to join God's wider mission in the world.

The second gift in Dozier's legacy is related to this mission: challenging lay persons to accept, as her first book names it, *The Authority of the Laity*. A former colleague of mine told me he found this title preposterous. Apparently the author (so he said) did not know all authority came from God. Of course Dozier knows, to quote her, that "religious authority is of God," and that this authority "comes with baptism." I am reminded that Stringfellow once named as a religious scandal the way American churches belittled "the authority that baptism vests in the laity." Clergy, Dozier freely acknowledges, are not always the culprits. "Clericalism"—a term which I define as distorted images of the status of clergy and laity alike—is widespread in the institutional church. Dozier observes that while human beings cannot take away the authority God has given us, "sinful human beings, however, can surrender it."[16]

Dozier has been an effective coach to many lay persons and lay groups: she names the traps explicitly, scolds incisively when necessary, and always encourages others to grasp their ministries more deeply. For example, she invites laity to ask why they think clergy ought "to know everything." She asks whether we believe that ministries done in the church are somehow more authentic than those done elsewhere. Like Underhill, she also challenges understandings of spirituality that are too restrictive. Dozier would agree with Joan Chittister that spirituality is "theology walking." Dozier, I believe, would add that the ground on which we stand is "holy ground," because God is "where we are." She cautions lay people against mistakenly thinking that they have "to go somewhere special" or "do something special" to find God. As long as this kind of thinking prevails, she warns, we will continue to see ourselves as "second-class citizens" and the work we do as second-class activities. Meanwhile Dozier, a skilled teacher of Bible study, invokes the saints to persevere in studying scripture, in prayer, and in worship.[17]

A third major aspect of Dozier's vision of the dream of God must not be overlooked or softened. While she admits that renewed attention to shared ministries is "a step forward," Dozier summons us to look beyond the everyday ministries of good deeds to addressing structural injustices in our society.

I think we have lost the capacity to dream great dreams. We reduce God to the personal, private, "spiritual" sphere of our lives, and ministry to personal, private, "spiritual" acts—a good deed here, a good deed there, a cup of cold water here, a loaf of freshly baked bread there, a prison visit here, a hospital call there, a light in a shelter here, a time with a troubled friend there. We see no need to challenge the systems that make these "ministries" necessary.

In this aspect of her theology, she reminds me of Stringfellow. While acknowledging that acts of charity are important, she encourages us to express the biblical legacy of love as justice. She preaches that individual care and outreach to the downtrodden while others of the world "trod them down some more" will not bring about the kingdom of God among the kingdoms of this world. Dozier longs for the day when we will pay more attention to the fact that ministry involves structural change. In that day, she notes, we will not only acknowledge the ministries of teachers, medical personnel, and social service workers, we will applaud the ministries of those who tackle difficult political, legislative, and economic issues. Meanwhile, Dozier concludes, "The terribly patient God still waits."[18]

Charles Willie

Charles Willie is an urban sociologist and university professor of education who for over forty-five years has been a national leader in efforts to reform and strengthen American public education. As a lay leader in the Episcopal Church, he has also worked to expose, understand, and overcome three interrelated "institutional sins" that are found in church and society: "racism, sexism, and elitism." Willie has helped others to see that "the oppression of anyone is the oppression of everyone." Verna Dozier's call for those who will seek to address structural social injustices in their everyday ministries is amply fulfilled in Willie's advocacy for racial justice, for reform of public education, and for full participation of all persons within the institutional church. Church and state have benefited from his powerful voice against discrimination in American society. For me Charles Willie's overall witness as a baptized Christian stands out as exemplary.[19]

Since his student days at Morehouse College, where in 1944 he joined the same freshman class as Martin Luther King, Jr., Willie has credited college president Benjamin E. Mays with shaping his moral world view and his advocacy of education. He describes Mays as teaching him that "a school should cultivate honest people who can be trusted, who are sensitive to that which is wrong in society, and who are willing to assume responsibility for correcting it." Willie's career offers eloquent testimony to the ways that he took his mentor's advice to heart. He interprets sociology as a humanity-centered discipline and describes himself as "an activist sociologist," a scholar who believes that "action without analysis can be as harmful as analysis without action."[20] Willie has pursued the goal of achieving justice in the nonviolent tradition of Martin Luther King. The title of Willie's first book, *Church Action in the World*

(1969), underscores the fact that his commitment to shaping public life includes active expectations of the church and of baptized Christians. When I reflect on those who exemplify the Baptismal Covenant's promise to "strive for justice and peace among all people, and respect the dignity of every human being" (BCP 305), Charles Willie comes to mind. As a well-known and respected educator, Willie has made important contributions to our knowledge of urban sociology and American education. Throughout his career he has often been called to serve as a consultant and expert witness in school desegregation cases across this country. In addition to being an influential college teacher and, since 1974, a professor at the Harvard University Graduate School of Education, Willie is a prolific author. Many of the books and articles that he published in the 1970s and 1980s focused on the dynamics of race, class, and race relations in public schools and in American higher education. As a sociologist Willie has also assessed the strength and character of black and white families, and has written about the lives of outstanding black scholars. A frequent public speaker, Willie has also contributed to understanding the complexities of American urban life by hosting a weekly public affairs television program. To this day his expertise continues to be sought by those who work for racial desegregation within public schools.

Willie has long been active in the parish, diocesan, and national life of the Episcopal Church. From 1970 to 1974 he served as the elected vice-president of the House of Deputies of the Episcopal Church's General Convention. The grandson of slaves, Willie has spoken of his gifts and achievements both in church and society as "outcomes of God's grace." His theology of ministry is summed up in his longtime advocacy of the priesthood of all believers. This, in fact, is the title of the sermon he preached at the 1974 Philadelphia ordinations of eleven women. On this occasion Willie drew explicit parallels between the civil rights movement and the women's movement, concluding that these women, like many African Americans, were "refusing to cooperate in their own oppression by remaining on the periphery of full participation in the church." In this sermon he also quoted theologian Martin Buber's belief that "human truth can be communicated only if one throws one's self into the process and answers for it with one's self." He concluded his sermon with words from the prayer book insisting that he, like others on that day, would "make no peace with oppression."[21]

These words proved prophetic. Shortly after the Philadelphia ordinations, Willie resigned from the House of Deputies, taking this step as an act of conscience to protest the refusal by the House of Bishops to hear directly from the women involved in Philadelphia. Willie did not resign, however, from church membership or parish involvement. Nor did he back away from the central moral commitment to act upon what he believed. In his vocation as an educational reformer and advocate for justice in the church and in society, he has sought to embody justice as love in action, seeking congruity in his words and in his works. For this lay leader "history, change and stability are equally important; we change that which harms and stabilize that which helps."[22] Expressing in our ministries the biblical legacy of love while tackling difficult social issues is demanding work for laity and clergy alike. Still, Willie persistently supports the dignity of all persons and proclaims the priesthood of all believers.

⌇ Postscript

My intent in this chapter has been to recover foundational biblical understandings of God's people and to review historical and recent changes in thinking about ministry. I have approached this story first by reviewing the history of terms and functional definitions of ministry, and then by moving on to envision ministry and ministers at work in the world by focusing on the contributions of four lay leaders.

Together this quartet of inspirational leaders who see the church broadly have given us a larger view of reality, a fuller landscape with resources for rediscovering laity as key agents of God's mission. They have drawn deeply upon biblical and other historical understandings of ministry. Evelyn Underhill envisioned spirituality in our daily lives as education for action. Verna Dozier has challenged us to accept the incarnate, God-given authority bestowed on us in baptism. And William Stringfellow and Charles Willie have faced directly into conflict and envisioned new possibilities for human community. The lives of these lay persons are incarnate, visible signs of God's activity in the world.

~ Chapter Four

Living with Controversy

When I tell new acquaintances that I am a historian, they often tell me that history is irrelevant. Many people do think history is boring, and others think the past should be left far behind in order to focus on the future. In general, we prefer to ignore history or think of it as a neutral topic that does not really have anything to do with our lives—until there is a serious problem. When a dispute arises, especially an argument or discussion about different practices or interpretations, history suddenly becomes a valuable ally. All sides and parties appeal to it, hauling out that familiar phrase, "But we've *always* done it this way!" Appealing to history is an age-old strategy: it was a standard practice in biblical times, during the English Reformation, in times of religious expansion like the founding of the Episcopal Church in America, and amid the vast social changes of the industrial revolution. And it persists in religious life today. Knowledge of history—insight from the past—becomes valuable as we struggle to live, grow, and change as people and as institutions.

One of my favorite stories about living with disagreement is about a synagogue that was in the midst of a very bitter conflict about the saying of the *Shema*, that most sacred moment in the Hebrew liturgy when the congregation says, "Hear, O Israel, the LORD is One God and you shall love him with all your heart, soul, and might." One group in the synagogue insisted that the congregation stand during the *Shema*, showing respect and reverence; another group, just as vehement, said they should sit in the posture of learning, as a symbol that they were being taught. Finally the rabbi took three standers and three sitters and went to see Mr. Finkelstein, the oldest living member of the original congregation, in a convalescent home.

One of the standers said, "Now, Mr. Finkelstein, surely when they had the *Shema* in those early days of the synagogue, you stood. Can you remember? Tell us and help us out of this impasse."

Mr. Finkelstein said, "I can't remember."

Then a person representing the sitters said, "Surely when that great moment of instruction came, you sat down to hear the *Shema*, 'Hear, O Israel.'"

Mr. Finkelstein said, "I can't remember."

Then the rabbi said, "Now, Mr. Finkelstein, you've got to put your mind to this question and tell us what it was like in those old, traditional days. Tell us what you remember. Members of our congregation are fighting each other, tearing each other apart. The congregation is divided and no one speaks to anybody."

"That," Mr. Finkelstein said, "I remember!"

Like Mr. Finkelstein, we tend to remember behaviors and not rationales. We may remember the passionate heat of a family argument, but we are not always sure what led to its resolution. At such times history can be a helpful resource, even though knowing how we have handled a situation in the past will not invariably suggest the best solution. It will, however, provide valuable information for us to consider as part of the context of our current disagreements. The philosopher Etienne Gilson once observed that history is the only laboratory we have for testing the consequences of our thoughts and actions. History opens for us the great vista of human experience. Through this lens we can view the wide range of accommodations that individuals and institutions have made in confronting difficult problems. We can also observe, with the hindsight of history, consequences of the various choices that they have made.

In our first chapter we observed the close kinship between tradition and change, noting that it is traditional for Christians to turn to history as a resource in making decisions. In the second chapter I selected among my touchstones in history several occasions when church leaders acted decisively. The perceptions these leaders had of tradition directly influenced the responses and contributions they made at these turning points. Similarly, in the previous chapter we observed how biblical understandings of ministry have been observed (or not) as part of the evolving ministry of lay persons.

In this chapter I want to look at three historic episodes when our ancestors in the Anglican church made hard choices about their religious identity. I have in mind three occasions when the church faced significant controversy among its members: the Elizabethan Settlement of religion in England during the second half of the sixteenth century, the official stance of the Episcopal Church during the American Civil War, and the Anglican theological response toward the end of the nineteenth century to modern critical teaching about evolution and the Bible. On the first occasion, our ancestors resolved difference and conflict in a spirit of conservative compromise, while on the second they officially ignored sharp differences in the name of church unity. On the third, they embraced with theological acuity the challenge of new ideas and ways of seeing the world.

The three episodes that I have chosen have each shaped, for good or ill, our institutional history as a church, and their legacies persist today. What resources do we have for addressing well-intended and vociferous religious parties as they contend for theological leadership in the life of the church? What lessons can we take from our Elizabethan ancestors? How did Episcopalians deal with the racial, political, and economic dimensions of slavery during a bloody Civil War? When traditional religious truths are seemingly challenged by modern scientific developments, what are we to believe? Whether we are considering Darwin's findings about evolution or today's new physics, how are we to imagine the mystery of creation? In short, what can we learn from the laboratory of history when vastly different world views clash?

To answer these questions, I want to begin with the basic Anglican method for dealing with pluralism, that of turning first to scripture and then to tradition. So before I explore my three historic episodes of conflict, I will turn first to what the New Testament reveals of differences, conflict, and dissent in the life of early Christian communities.

∾ Conflict in Early Christian Communities

We should be reassured to learn that it is not a new experience for the church to struggle with the problems as well as the advantages of living with difference and disagreement. From the start, those who came to follow Jesus after the first Easter were members of multilingual and multicultural communities. Many were Greek-speaking Jews and other residents of the Roman Empire who drew upon the customs and peoples of the Middle East, the Mediterranean basin, and Asia Minor to create their new communities of faith. Scholars now believe that Jesus was raised near an interesting mixture of cultures, close to a thriving and sophisticated urban center. Moreover, Jesus was completely immersed in the Judaism of that time, a faith that was diverse and full of lively quarrels and debates. Some modern biblical scholars also believe Jesus was trilingual, with knowledge of Aramaic, Hebrew, and enough Hellenistic Greek to function well in the market culture of the cities. The Jerusalem of Jesus' day, although a Jewish city, was a center of Middle Eastern cultures, commerce, and wealth, inhabited by different races and cultures that did not often intersect or understand one another's ways: Greek and Roman merchants, bureaucrats, soldiers and their families, as well as Syrians, Persians, Arabs, Phoenicians, and Egyptians. This was the city toward which Jesus purposefully walked in the final months of his earthly life.

This wide diversity at the origins of Christianity was further complicated by the politics of living in the Roman Empire, although not because Roman authorities persecuted the earliest followers of Jesus for their beliefs. The Roman world of Jesus' day was cynically tolerant of all religions and devoted to none. Those affiliated with the young Christian movement, like all other inhabitants of Roman antiquity, were responsible for meeting the imperial requirements (typically taxation) of Roman authorities. The diverse followers of Jesus faced the difficult and complex question of how they could exist within the Roman Empire while maintaining that Jesus (and not the emperor) is Lord.

The earliest followers of the Jesus movement were also part of a wildly variegated group of village dwellers, wanderers, and urbanites. From the beginning of the second century, it is possible to speak of "Christianities" as a plural reality, with regional variations and different sects of Christianity present even in the same city. This is one of the reasons I like to think of the day of Pentecost as an ecclesiastical miracle, as men and women assembled from different cultures and tongues found that they could actually understand one another. The Pentecost story not only conveys a miracle, it provides an effective metaphor for the developing story of the church as it unfolds in the New Testament.

The Pauline epistles provide us with additional insights into the internal struggles of early Christian communities, particularly the churches in Corinth and in Rome. Corinth was a Greco-Roman city famous for its large temple of Apollo and its rich variety of popular religious cults and gods, including the Persian god Mithras, whose birth was celebrated on December 25, and the popular Egyptian goddess Isis. It is not surprising that members of the church in Corinth faced internal and external issues of unity and conformity alongside those of freedom and diversity. Paul's letters to the Corinthians addressed many disputes and divisions, including the contentious factions that Paul believed had developed among religious leaders, with some following Apollos and others Cephas, and still others acting on their own authority. There were debates about the present benefits of the resurrection, the validity of spiritual gifts, and the individual rather than community benefits of these gifts.

Part of Paul's response to this diverse religious community suggests that differences can actually be constructive. He writes, "There have to be factions among you, for only so will it become clear who among you are genuine" (1 Corinthians 11:19). In other words, Paul believes that conflicts and divisive situations can clarify and build up the church, provided that the basic ground rule of love and charity prevails among its members. We may not always remember that the famous Pauline passage on love originated as a response to tensions generated by living with diversity in a Christian community:

> Love is patient; love is kind; love is not envious or boastful or arrogant or rude. It does not insist on its own way; it is not irritable or resentful; it does not rejoice in wrongdoing, but rejoices in the truth. It bears all things, believes all things, hopes all things, endures all things. Love never ends. (1 Corinthians 13:4-8)

Living with difference was also a central component in Paul's letter to the Christian church in Rome. Marked divisions in this early Christian community included struggles over class and status, as well as spirited controversies over diet and ritual observances that reflect the fundamental challenge of how Jewish Christians could get along with Gentile Christians. Paul calls them to mutually supportive relationships which, founded as they are in baptism, remove our need or desire to judge others. Pleas for charity, for envisioning the community as "one body in Christ" (12:5), and for reaching out to "welcome one another" (15:7) abound in this epistle. Here Paul insists that Christians are to welcome difference and variety because God in Christ has done so. When the community's internal relationships are characterized by charity, differences can be embraced within the body of believers.

In short, embracing difference and coming to terms with diversity have always been components of life in Christian community. It is erroneous to think that the church today is somehow unique, that rowdy innovators and dissenters, "traditionalists" and "postmodernists," are something brand new rather than part of the history we have inherited. Religiously speaking, the age we live in is no more unruly than any other. There never was an early

Christian "golden age;" nor did late twentieth-century people like ourselves invent the religious mayhem that breaks out in struggles for religious unity. From the beginning Christians have differed over what the Holy Spirit asks of the church. It is to three such episodes in this history of turmoil and dissent that I now wish to turn.

∿ Resolving Conflict through Compromise: The Elizabethan Settlement

From time to time I am asked a standard question by those in confirmation classes or inquirers' groups who are trying to sort out our historical roots: "Did Henry VIII found the Church of England?" "No," I typically reply, "his daughter, Queen Elizabeth I, did!"

Of course it is not that simple, but I stand by my response. When it comes to thinking about the most influential figure who encouraged by her actions (and inaction) a comprehensive structure for the Church of England, that figure is clearly Elizabeth I, who ruled England from 1558 to 1603. Historians have called the "Elizabethan Settlement" of religion the central achievement of her reign. "Settlement" refers to the guidelines that were established early in Elizabeth's reign for the worship, governance, and theological character of an English church that would balance tradition and the need for reform, and Catholic sacramental structure with Protestant theological understandings. The story of how this compromise came about is marked by danger, foreign and political intrigue, and emphatic leadership from the young queen and her chief administrator, William Cecil. It also involves contentious clergy and laity with varied backgrounds and strongly-held opinions. In short, the story of the Elizabethan Settlement, like that of Pentecost, is somewhat miraculous. It is astounding that anything like a clear and durable identity for the English church eventually emerged from the religious turmoil, widespread theological differences, and political chaos of the sixteenth century. This story is also formative for the character of what we in a later century call Anglicanism. The major elements of this historic epic make for compelling drama. Act I involves setting the stage for the early settlement victory and exploring its two central legislative achievements, while in Act II Elizabeth Tudor takes center stage as the doctrinal implications of her settlement begin to unfold. Act III allows us to hear from two theological defenders of the settlement—John Jewel and Richard Hooker—and to conclude the story with its legacies, achievements, and mixed blessings. Along the way, it is important to remember that our spiritual ancestors (like ourselves) lived in an age of bewildering religious complexity, and hindsight can give the retelling of any historical tale a false impression of inevitability.

With the accession of the twenty-five-year-old Virgin Queen, little in Tudor society seemed sure or settled, but expectation was high. To the reformers—those Protestants who were seeking to restore to the church a belief in the centrality of scripture—Elizabeth's reign promised the miraculous. For when the Catholic queen, Mary Tudor, died on November 17, 1558, she had been attempting with her minister Cardinal Reginald Pole (who died the same day) to bring about the English church's reunion with Rome. At Mary's death bonfires were lit by rejoicing reformers in London. On the European continent the news of the death of "Bloody Mary" warmed the hearts of English exiles who had fled her repressive rule, which had included the burning of some three hundred Protestants. I can imagine these reformers thinking, "Surely this was the Lord's doing!"

Sixteenth-century England already had experienced abrupt and dramatic shifts in religious formation, beginning with Henry VIII's severing of jurisdictional relations with the papacy in the 1530s and Thomas Cranmer's gradual introduction of reformed worship during the short reign of Henry's male heir, Edward VI, through Mary Tudor's partially successful attempts to win the English people back to Roman Catholicism. So change, rather than stability, was the norm. Much now depended on the character of the new monarch, Elizabeth, whose mother Anne Boleyn had been beheaded, who had been declared a bastard when she was three, whose father had died when she was thirteen, and who at twenty had been imprisoned in the Tower of London.

An additional factor that further complicated the prospects for religious stability was the influence of reformed theology and worship on the Continent. Returning exiles, accustomed to the more reformed liturgical traditions and customs found in many German and Swiss cities, had high hopes for moving beyond the reforms and customs of Edward VI's reign. A few also had journeyed to John Calvin's Geneva, among them John Knox, a Scottish reformer and devoted Calvinist. In 1558 Knox wrote a treatise asserting that government by a woman is contrary to nature and to God. While he had in mind Catholic queens like Mary of Guise in France and Mary Tudor in England, his tract—*The First Blast of the Trumpet against the Monstrous Regiment of [Ruling] Women*—did not endear him to Elizabeth Tudor. Nor did the returning Calvinists welcome royal interference in church governance. Throughout her reign Elizabeth would have to contend with the growing theological influence of these Presbyterians, as they came to be called. Another threat at the start of her reign was that of diplomatic isolation, if not military invasion, from allied Catholic monarchies in France, Scotland, and Spain who sympathized with Mary Tudor. So few could have predicted that within a year of her coronation the young queen, along with her lay advisors and bishops, would peacefully establish a lasting base for the church in England. Elizabeth's religious choices needed to be as broadly based as possible in order to avoid a variety of extremes. She did not wish to antagonize the Roman Catholics unnecessarily, either at home or abroad, and the anti-monarchical influences of Geneva were neither appealing nor helpful. Although the queen needed the support and clerical leadership of the returning Marian exiles, their reformed theological views and expectations were generally more radical than her own. Few of her leaders shared her loyalty to the Henrician Catholic and conservative Edwardian faith in which she was raised. Although there is disagreement among historians, it appears that Elizabeth probably preferred Cranmer's conservative prayer book of 1549 to its successor, the more Protestant and reformed 1552 *Book of Common Prayer*. It was in this context of conflicting expectations, sharply diverse religious beliefs, and diplomatic dangers that Elizabeth and her chief ministers seized the moment to accomplish their goals.

Less than six months after her coronation, the framework of the religious settlement was in place. By the spring of 1559, the Act of Supremacy and a revised prayer book enforced by an Act of Uniformity had been prepared, debated, and enacted. While it would take time for these two pillars of the Elizabethan Settlement to shape conventional religious life in England, the speed and ease of this settlement were astounding. For support the queen had turned to moderates like herself, who were products of the break with Rome and skilled survivors in the political art of compromise. Sir William Cecil, the queen's principal secretary and longtime adviser, was the chief architect of the religious settlement in Parliament. The queen selected Matthew

Parker—a moderate reformer who had lived in obscurity during Mary's reign—to lead her church as Archbishop of Canterbury. Since Mary Tudor's Catholic bishops refused to cooperate with Elizabeth, most of the Elizabethan bishops were of necessity drawn from the more experienced ranks of returning Protestant exiles. Although these convinced reformers were largely devoted to their new queen, they could and would prove difficult. Yet at first the religious legislation of 1559 allowed their hopes and expectations of further reform to survive.

The first and most essential component of the settlement, one that would in time distinctively shape Anglican tradition, was its reaffirmation of royal supremacy. The Act of Supremacy confirmed Henry VIII's break with Rome, repealed the heresy legislation of Mary Tudor's reign, and required religious and civil ministers to take an oath of supremacy to Elizabeth. The queen's title became "Supreme Governor," rather than (as under Henry VIII and his immediate successors) "Supreme Head" of the realm. The language shift here is a prime example of flexible Elizabethan statecraft. The title of "governor" was more palatable both to those Roman Catholics who recognized the pope as head of the church and to those Protestant reformers who believed that the head of Christendom was Christ alone.

The Act of Supremacy did not *directly* substitute the authority of the crown for that of the pope because Tudor England was not a theocracy—a state led by a divine ruler. The model of governance was rather that of a unified commonwealth with a chief governor for both the civil and ecclesiastical spheres. Royal supremacy allowed Elizabeth and her successors to maintain and protect a reformed religion in England without interference from papal or other foreign religious powers, like Spain. This legacy of geographical autonomy would be drawn upon by North Americans in the eighteenth century as they sought to establish the Protestant Episcopal Church in the United States of America.

The second pillar of the Elizabethan Settlement was a newly revised *Book of Common Prayer*. Use of the 1559 prayer book, like its two predecessors from Edward VI's reign, was legally mandated by the Act of Uniformity. Thus English clergy were to use it for all public worship, while laity (as in 1552) were required to attend church on Sundays and major holy days. This legislation was designed to return English worship to the genius of Thomas Cranmer's liturgical tradition as it had been first established in 1549 and further reformed in the prayer book of 1552. The proposed Elizabethan *Book of Common Prayer* was based on its 1552 predecessor, with a few modifications to the communion service. By the way, the authorization of this new prayer book barely passed; in the House of Lords, the Act of Uniformity succeeded by only two votes. The opposition, led by Mary Tudor's soon-to-be-replaced Catholic bishops and by conservative laymen, came close to blocking even this moderate settlement. It may be reassuring for us to recall today that heated debates and close votes on the adoption of new prayer books are far from new to our tradition!

The changes made in the 1559 Elizabethan prayer book underscore Elizabeth's sagacity in providing a regular form of worship that still left room for broad interpretation and adaptation. Catholic sacramental structure and Protestant theological understandings alike were confirmed. The most telling example was a decisive and effective use of the tradition whereby phrases that had been said at the delivery of the bread and then of the wine in the two prior liturgies were joined. The new text read:

> Hear us, O merciful Father, we beseech thee; and grant
> that we receiving these thy creatures of bread and wine,
> according to thy Son our Savior Jesu Christ's holy insti-
> tution, in remembrance of his death and passion, may
> be partakers of his most blessed Body and Blood: who in
> the same night that he was betrayed, took bread, and
> when he had given thanks, he brake it, and gave it to his
> disciples, saying, Take, eat, this is my body which is
> given for you. Do this in remembrance of me. (*The Book
> of Common Prayer*, 1559)

Such a combination allowed those who held a variety of
theological beliefs to participate in a communion service
that could be understood both as a sacrifice and a remembrance. The effect was to allow the possibility not only of
prior English perspectives, but also of Catholic, Lutheran,
and Swiss reformed interpretations of the communion
service. One astute historian has accurately described the
1559 prayer book as a "Protestant creed dressed up in the
time-honored vestments of Catholicism."[1] It is not surprising that William Cecil and other ministers praised the
queen's spirit of moderation and willingness to compromise.

Elizabeth's attempted compromises on the use of clerical vestments (like the white linen gown called the surplice)
and other customary church appointments (like crucifixes
and candlesticks) were less successful. The Act of Uniformity contained a controversial proviso that returned clerical
dress and church furniture to the standard use of 1549,
early in Edward VI's reign. Unlike their queen, most Elizabethan reformers wanted "popish" objects, vestments, and
practices not mentioned in scripture—using the sign of the
cross in baptism and kneeling to receive communion, for
example—removed. At stake were not only local parish

customs and devotional habits, but the disappearance of Catholic images, altars, and vestments from the churches. Protestant reformers were hopeful (though misguided) that the queen would soon welcome further simplifications in dress. Arguments over clerical dress and church furnishings may sound frivolous, but I have witnessed explosive conflicts over similar matters in parishes I have attended.

Despite these regulations, a great deal of variety remained in local Elizabethan congregations. Some churches emphasized the ceremonial aspects, with ministers clothed in full vestments (perhaps a cope, at least a surplice), with hymns and other music, and with the congregation walking forward from the nave to the chancel to receive the wafer and wine, kneeling or standing. Other local parishes were more austere. Such parishes used simpler ornaments: a minister in a scholar's gown, no music except for congregational singing of the psalms in a plain meter, and a table moved into the midst of the people, from which they received the bread and wine either standing or sitting (the posture that some reformers thought accorded best with scriptural warrants).

In a characteristically English fashion, the first phase of the Elizabethan Settlement established the *legal* grounds for the governance and worship of the church long before turning to specific matters of doctrine. The second phase was longer and much more difficult. In 1563, Elizabeth stood at what has been described as an "ecclesiastical crossroads." Few of her contemporaries believed that the 1559 settlement would endure without further doctrinal and liturgical reform. Zealous reformers were called by the initially derogatory label of "Puritan," a term that was used to describe those whose focus on the Bible and desire to rid the church of popish superstitions distinguished them from their more lukewarm contemporaries.

When the first synod, or convocation, of Elizabethan clergy gathered in 1563, proposals were introduced (and initially approved) that would have moved England significantly toward more radical, Swiss-inspired reforms. One provision, for instance, would have outlawed the use of pipe organs and other musical instruments in worship because they lacked scriptural warrants. Another, predictably, called for simpler clerical dress. In the same year, a popular bill targeting English Catholics was initially approved by Parliament. This measure, had it gained Elizabeth's approval, would have imposed the death penalty on anyone twice refusing the oath of supremacy. Although she effectively suppressed such measures, they reflect the tightly wound popular temper of the times, with its search for doctrinal precision, discipline, and conformity.

It took twelve years after the authorization of the 1559 prayer book to reach agreement on a moderate statement of doctrinal discipline. This statement, called the Thirty-Nine Articles, was largely the work of Tudor bishops and was based upon doctrinal affirmations going back to Henry VIII's reign, though it waited until 1571 for royal assent. The Thirty-Nine Articles were briefer, more conservative, less dogmatic, and more open to interpretation than their English predecessors and the doctrinal statements of Roman Catholics, Lutherans, and Calvinists. At least one-third of the articles affirmed Catholic and ecumenical teachings, others reflected common Protestant emphases, and the remainder addressed prayer book understandings of the eucharist or dealt with distinctly English matters like royal supremacy. Thus Anglican theology under Elizabeth Tudor was a hybrid containing features that were broadly Catholic, Lutheran, Zwinglian, and Calvinist. One church historian describes the Thirty-Nine Articles as:

fruitful soil for the growth of [the church's] distinctive comprehensiveness. In an age when ecclesiastical guards were busy shutting doors to theological alternatives, the Elizabethan reformers left a remarkable number of doors ajar.[2]

The Thirty-Nine Articles have left Anglicans today with a legacy of moderation, opposition to absolutism, and openmindedness. Perhaps this Elizabethan tolerance is one reason that Episcopalians and other Anglicans are often constructive participants in modern-day ecumenical conversations.

As a summary statement of doctrine, the Thirty-Nine Articles are an important component of the Elizabethan Settlement, while their spirit of moderation also reflects Anglican identity. Elizabeth repudiated attempts by over-zealous reformers to require all laity to swear allegiance to these articles, a step that would have moved the Church of England toward being a confessional church like the Lutheran or Reformed. Although they were important to the ordering of clerical leadership, the articles did not have the same legal force as prayer book worship. Clergy were asked to conform to them, while all members of the church were enjoined by the Act of Uniformity to participate in the "common prayers" of the church. Consequently, doctrinal precision and enforced theological uniformity did not become key factors in Anglican identity.

The moderate temperament of early Elizabethan Anglicanism was decidedly shaped by the queen herself. Elizabeth's exact religious opinions are still the subject of debate, although I suspect her personal preferences tended toward what we today might describe as Anglo-Catholic ceremonial. Her official approach to religious diversity, however, was direct: she would not force or inquire into the consciences of others. Elizabeth was fond of noting that she did not seek "windows" into her subjects' souls. Instead, like Thomas Cranmer, she sought to seek agreement first by persuasion rather than by coercion, as one of her ministers noted: "Consciences are not to be forced, but to be won and reduced by force of truth, by the aid of time and the use of all good means of instruction or persuasion."[3] With general forbearance and leniency, Elizabeth attempted to reserve capital punishment for treason and direct threats to the security of the realm. This is not to suggest that the queen believed in religious freedom, any more than others of that day. She did, however, choose to stand against contemporary pressures to enact repressive legislation against nonconformists. For most of her reign she also successfully opposed—until political and diplomatic pressures escalated in the 1580s—punitive legislation against Roman Catholics.

Elizabeth's major theological defenders and interpreters, John Jewel and Richard Hooker, shared her conviction that religious beliefs were to be won by force of learning, not of legislation. Jewel, a moderate reformer and bishop, provided a classical statement of Anglican identity in his *Apology for the Church of England*, published in 1562. He emphasized that the Church of England was not founded on new doctrine, but continued in the essential catholicism of the faith except on those points where Rome "erred" and departed from "God's Word." Jewel appealed to the authority of scripture itself as well as the theologians of the patristic period, roughly defined as the first five hundred years of Christian history.

Like Jewel before him, Richard Hooker also cited scripture and patristic scholarship to illustrate and defend the English church's claims to catholicity. In one pungent sentence he argues that theologically the church in England distances itself from the absolutist claims of both papal Rome and Calvinist Geneva: "Two things there are which trouble greatly these later times; one that the church of Rome cannot, another that Geneva will not, err."[4] Hooker's great contribution was to construct a theological framework that grounded the church in the authority of scripture, reason, and tradition. While not disputing the supremacy of the Bible, his method gave room for various interpretations and applications of scripture in church life and teaching. Indeed, Hooker directly defended religious diversity by appealing to the pervasive character and finality of God's abundant mercy, and warned against hastily condemning others for differing religious understandings by citing St. Paul:

> Be it that Cephas hath one interpretation, and Apollos hath another: that Paul is of this mind, and Barnabas of that. If this offend you, the fault is yours. Carry peaceable minds, and you may have comfort by this variety. Now the God of Peace give you peaceable minds, and turn it to your everlasting comfort.[5]

Elizabeth would have approved of any sermon that encouraged her subjects to be peaceable!

Anglicans have inherited from Jewel and Hooker, as well as from Elizabeth I, a preference both for moderation and breadth in theology along with a reluctance to define the mysteries of salvation too closely. One way of describing this stance has been to refer to Anglican theology as a *via media*, or middle way, between Roman Catholic and Protestant theologies. This phrase, which was first employed by seventeenth-century Anglican divines, needs cautious use. It can be a helpful image for interpreting Anglican identity if we understand that the center of the *via media* signifies a substantive core of theological conviction. Our Elizabethan ancestors did not simply choose a midpoint between extremes, nor did they idealize either centrism or neutrality. The danger they saw in religious extremism was its untempered zeal, not its commitment to the faith. From Cranmer and Hooker onward, English theologians labored to bring forth a church that was a true bearer of God's word and vision. At the center there was, as Elizabeth once aptly asserted, "only one Jesus Christ, and all the rest is a dispute about trifles."[6] Guided by a pragmatic and conservative spirit of compromise, Elizabeth and her religious leaders adroitly faced into theological controversy and emerged with a framework and methodology that sought to encompass all members of England's commonwealth.

We could interpret the Elizabethan Settlement and its struggle for religious identity and stability as a success story about living with controversy, and in many ways this is correct. Among its achievements was the difficult move from a religion of custom to one of conviction. The settlement also fostered a growing affection for a prayer book that, with a few modifications, would survive in English use into the twentieth century.

There were, of course, aspects of the Elizabethan Settlement that were far from popular. Indeed, part of the settlement was its "unsettled" character, its openness to a wide latitude of belief and practice. This did not please everyone. Puritans chafed at a "halfly-reformed" church and were increasingly outspoken in their attacks upon the queen's religious authority. Many English Catholics, called "recusants" for their refusal to attend services of the established church, practiced the old faith despite penal laws increasingly enforced against them in the latter half of Elizabeth's reign. For them, the English reformation was a disaster; for Puritans it was unfinished. Elizabeth's insistence from the 1570s onward that further religious reform was a closed subject drew increasing opposition from many quarters. Religious controversy continued throughout her reign, contributing to tensions that by the middle of the seventeenth century (and under less adept royal leadership) would lead to an English civil war. An additional though unintended lesson that we might learn from the Elizabethan effort to shape a church amid religious controversy is that it is difficult, even potentially dangerous, to try to freeze developmental progress in church life. Change, as Richard Hooker taught, is a natural part of it.

～ Ignoring Conflict:
The American Civil War

Unlike the story of our Elizabethan ancestors, who laid the foundations for reformed worship and governance in England by settling conflict through compromise, the story of the Episcopal Church's response to the American Civil War (1861–1865) provides one of the clearest examples of ignoring reality and bypassing conflict. Our church backed away from this civil crisis, with its immense suffering, seemingly determined to overlook in the name of church unity both the divisive character of the war and the issue of slavery. I want to look at this complicated moment in social and religious history, with its mixed bag of intentions and consequences, to see what lessons it holds for our identity as a people of faith today.

"A country is the things it wants to see." Thus Robert Pinsky, the American poet laureate, wrote about the shaping of our national identity in *An Explanation of America*.[7] How we choose to explain ourselves is related to what we remember. Since we naturally do not remember everything, the emphasis here needs to be on what we *selectively* choose to remember. This is a complex matter, especially in times of civil turmoil. Most church history texts do not dwell upon the Episcopal Church during the Civil War, despite the revival of popular interest in this period through recent television documentaries and movies. Furthermore, the impact of decisions made by religious leaders are generally not covered in popular histories, either, so it is not easy to investigate how people of faith responded to the central issue of slavery in American society.

At the center of this story is the fact that the Episcopal Church, unlike other major American Protestant denominations, officially chose *not* to speak out on slavery or on the morality of the war itself. What it did choose to address was the need for church unity, for holding northern and southern Episcopalians together. Thus in 1895 a bishop could write approvingly of the church's stance of "loyalty for the North, conciliation for the South, and the clerical avoidance of purely political questions—a stand which earned for the Church public respect and confidence."[8] Writing almost a century later, a historian and Episcopal priest calls it a "morally tepid" response:

> Unlike other major American denominations—the Methodists, Baptists and Presbyterians—our church never officially divided over the issues of slavery or Civil War. In the face of the cruelties of human bondage, the oppression of an entire race, and a war that eventually would free the slaves and end an institution that the civilized world of the nineteenth century abhorred...the Episcopal Church in 1862 decided that preserving its institutional integrity and reconciling divided elements within the United States was more essential than endorsing whole-heartedly a struggle...recognized as a moral and just one.[9]

Both historians agree that the dominant goal of Episcopal Church leaders during the Civil War was preserving church unity, but they diverge sharply in their interpretations of the moral and political implications.

The Episcopal Church was not alone in its reluctance to talk directly about the moral, political, and constitutional implications of the nation's most pressing problem: chattel slavery. After all, the House of Representatives, from 1836 to 1844, upheld a gag rule preventing members from discussing antislavery proposals. From the 1830s onward, Congressman John Quincy Adams—who called slavery "the great and foul stain upon the North American Union"—led the fight to discuss the elimination of slavery on the floor of the House. In effect, national leaders of the Episcopal Church exercised their own unofficial gag rule, at least in the House of Bishops. During the Civil War they endeavored to live with controversy by denying not only the deep causative conflict over slavery, but also the war itself. The famous Episcopal preacher Phillips Brooks wrote his observations of the bishops' deliberations during the 1862 General Convention:

> It was ludicrous, if not so sad, to see those old gentlemen sitting there for fourteen days, trying to make out whether there was a war going on or not, and whether if there was it would be safe for them to say so.[10]

Obviously there were powerful forces and patterns at work that led up to this patent denial of reality and kept the church from dealing more directly with the moral issues at hand. What was the Episcopal Church's record in addressing slavery prior to the Civil War? Were members of the church divided in their support of slavery? What rationales for official actions by bishops in the North and in the South can be found in the 1862 Pastoral Letters issued by *two* Houses of Bishops: one from the Episcopal Church in the United States of America, and the other from the Episcopal

Church in the Confederate States of America? What made appeals for unity successful not only in 1862, but also at the war's end in 1865? How did the actions taken (and not taken) by the Episcopal Church influence the church's postwar ministry with African Americans?

In 1623 the first African slaves were baptized in the Church of England in Virginia. Since southern colonial Anglicans upheld the rights of slaveholders over those of their slaves, whose duties included absolute obedience to their owners, there was some debate about the wisdom of baptizing slaves. Virginia's laws (emulated by other southern colonies) emphasized that baptism did not mean manumission, or freedom from bondage. The liberating Pauline baptismal formula found in Galatians 3:28, proclaiming that "there is no longer slave or free," apparently was set aside by slaveholders. In 1727, the bishop of London advised colonial clergy under his authority that baptism does not affect the "outward condition" of free persons or of slaves. On the other hand, there was also little debate about the desirability of religious instruction for slaves, although practices varied widely. The Society for the Propagation of the Gospel in Foreign Parts (the SPG) worked from 1701 until the American Revolution to advance the religious education of slaves. Throughout the eighteenth and early nineteenth centuries evangelical Episcopalians developed active and largely white-led ministries to slaves through Sunday schools and plantation chapels. In white parishes, galleries and other special sections were set aside for slaves and freed African Americans.

In antebellum America, the Episcopal Church was a small but visible body, enrolling a tiny percentage of Americans (1.3 percent), approximately one hundred forty-six thousand in all by 1860. On the eve of the Civil War there were an estimated thirty-five thousand

African-American Episcopalians living in the South. Many of these were in South Carolina, where one hundred fifty congregations of slaves worshiped under white control. These numbers correspond to the important fact that, as the southern Episcopal bishops reported in 1862, "a very large proportion of the great slaveholders" were Episcopalians. One of these was Leonidas Polk, a bishop who owned four hundred slaves. There were also a few congregations of African-American Episcopalians in southern and northern cities where free and other blacks worshiped. Absalom Jones founded St. Thomas African Episcopal Church in Philadelphia in 1794. Other churches were founded in urban areas, including New York City, Newark, Baltimore, Savannah, and Charleston. By 1865, twenty-five African Americans had been ordained. Clearly, members of the Episcopal Church, like its colonial predecessor, had direct experience before the onset of the Civil War in addressing the issue of slavery and the religious formation of slaves and free African Americans.[11]

Northern and southern Episcopalians also held divergent points of view. Although the Episcopal Church did not divide over slavery, as did the Baptists (in 1846), the Presbyterians (in 1837 and 1861), and the Methodists (in 1843 and 1844), there was abundant internal controversy. From the 1830s on, a number of Episcopal clergy and laity belonged to the American Anti-Slavery Society. Some Episcopalians advocated outright abolition, others gradual emancipation, and still others, including William H. Seward and Salmon P. Chase, sought to prohibit slavery's extension into new territories and states. Episcopal laymen William and John Jay (descendants of the Revolutionary leader John Jay) were active abolitionists, as was Alexander Crummell, the talented black intellectual leader and Episcopal priest who in the 1850s served as a missionary to

Liberia. One of the most vigorous Episcopal preachers against slavery was Phillips Brooks. He described from the pulpit the "two natures" in America, one built with "magnified labor" and freedom, and the other dependent upon slavery and a new "feudalism." Brooks correctly asserted that "the history of our country for many years is the history of how these two elements of American life approached collision."[12]

There were Episcopalians in the North as well as the South who firmly upheld the legitimacy of slavery. One 1861 apologetic, entitled *American Slavery Distinguished from the Slavery of English Theorists and Justified by the Law of Nature*, was written by the Rev. Samuel Seabury of New York City (the grandson and namesake of the first American Episcopal bishop). Another influential pamphlet was authored by the bishop of Vermont, John H. Hopkins. This treatise—*A Scriptural, Ecclesiastical, and Historical View of Slavery from the Days of the Patriarch Abraham to the 19th Century*—emphasized the "blessings" of slavery and described how, under southern slaveholders, these are "the happiest laborers in the world." Like many others of his age, Hopkins pointed directly to specific biblical texts and arguments as traditional sanctions for slavery and emphasized the need to convert slaves to Christianity. Hopkins, who would serve as Presiding Bishop throughout most of the Civil War, was a friend of other bishops who sympathized with slavery—notably the slaveholder Leonidas Polk (first consecrated in 1838 as a missionary bishop to Arkansas and the Indian Territory, and after 1841 the first bishop of Louisiana) and Stephen Elliott of Georgia. Polk, who shared close associations with Episcopalians in the North, accepted in 1861 a military commission as a general in the Confederate armies. He defended the "cause" of the Confederacy as "nothing less than the preservation of the purity of religious truth."[13] As Abraham Lincoln aptly noted in his second inaugural address: "Both [sides] read the same Bible, and pray to the same God: and each invokes His aid against the other."

What then actually happened in the Episcopal Church when war was declared? How did bishops in the South and in the North describe their actions? Bishops in southern dioceses from 1861 on began to organize themselves into a separate church. This was apparently overlooked as leaders of the Protestant Episcopal Church in the United States of America (PECUSA) gathered in October of 1862 for General Convention. When the roll was called in the House of Bishops, bishops from southern dioceses were quietly marked as "absent." Despite the strong voices of some bishops and other clergy who conspicuously supported the Union and wanted to protest actions of bishops in the South, the official church stance was studied silence and, for some, overt sympathy for their brothers and friends in the South. The PECUSA bishops' Pastoral Letter emphasized, most of all, patriotism and loyalty to the Union. The sharpest language, presented with the prayer book's indictment, was directed at the southern states' secession from the constituted government:

> Ever since our Church had her Litany, we have been praying for deliverance "from sedition, privy conspiracy, and rebellion." And now that all the three are upon us...shall we refuse to tell you in what light we regard that gigantic evil?

Secession from the Union, not slavery, was named as the causative issue. In fact, slavery was not directly mentioned in this long Pastoral Letter. The only oblique reference called upon the loyalty of church members "of all classes and conditions" to support the Government in its "rightful control of its laws."[14] Once war came, differences among northern Episcopalians on how to address slavery were seemingly set aside, with emphasis placed on preserving the Union. Although there were exceptions (notably in Pennsylvania), editors of some diocesan newspapers praised Episcopal leaders for not being like the "chief political preachers" of division in other denominations. Accordingly, at the 1862 General Convention, the division of the Episcopal Church was not officially recognized.

Meanwhile, the bishops in the southern states joined their dioceses as independent members of a newly constituted Protestant Episcopal Church in the Confederate States of America (PECCSA). The Pastoral Letter from the PECCSA House of Bishops—adopted in November of 1862 when members met in their first General Council—spoke directly of being "forced by the providence of God to separate ourselves" from the Episcopal Church in the North, although in most matters it remained "in entire harmony" with the doctrine, discipline, and worship of that church. The reason for separation was not institutional disagreement but the "cruel war...desolating our homes and firesides." This Pastoral Letter went on to describe the difficult missionary challenges facing them, calling the "religious instruction" of slaves the "greatest work" ahead:

> The time has come when the Church should press more urgently than she has hitherto done upon her laity, the solemn fact, that the slaves of the South are not so much property, but are a sacred trust committed to us, as a people, to be prepared for the work which God may have for them to do, in the future. While under this tutelage He freely gives to us their labor, but expects us to give back to them that religious and moral instruction which is to elevate them in the scale of Being.

The letter further asserted that "not only our spiritual but our national life is wrapped up in their [the slaves'] welfare. With them we stand or fall."[15] The sincerity of this appeal is clear and genuine, as were the religious convictions of Episcopalians who were military leaders in the Confederate armies, among them Robert E. Lee, Leonidas Polk, William Nelson Pendleton (later Lee's rector in Virginia), and William Porcher DuBose, who would emerge in years after the war as a prominent Episcopal theologian. In the postwar years, as during the war, the personal faith of influential southern leaders would serve as a source and symbol of self-esteem and ongoing strength.

With separation from the Union, not slavery, named as the primary issue, and with both Houses of Bishops declaring their affectionate ties with one another, it is not surprising that when war ended in 1865 most Episcopal leaders emphasized ecclesial reconciliation and harmony. In practice the issue of slavery had divided the Episcopal Church during the Civil War jurisdictionally, geographically, politically, and liturgically (specifically in the prayers for leaders of the government). Yet postwar leaders hastened to repair and then deny signs of the breach. Before the 1865 General Convention, Presiding Bishop Hopkins wrote to assure his southern brothers of a cordial welcome. During the Convention, southern deputations were welcomed back (all eleven dioceses returned within the year), the PECCSA consecration of Bishop Hooker Wilmer of Alabama was accepted, and consents were given for the bishop-elect of Tennessee. Bishop Hopkins worked to ensure that the 1865 Pastoral Letter did not directly address the issue of slavery, despite the fact that this Pastoral was written the same year as the Thirteenth Amendment to the Constitution abolishing it. After the 1865 General Convention, the official mood was one of celebration and denial. As a preacher from Trinity Parish, New York City, proclaimed:

> Brethren, our Church has never been divided. Our enemies said that it was, but they were wrong. The storm of war deranged for a time our means of intercourse, and thereby necessarily suspended our rules of canonical action, but the life and heart were one....After what has occurred, no one can with truth affirm that the Episcopal Church has known a schism. We trust in the Lord for the future, as we trusted in Him in the past. The Church has never been divided.[16]

This is a clear example of making history say what we want it to say, a public proclamation of historical revision. The "gigantic evil" of sedition, named in the northern bishops' 1862 Pastoral Letter, was forgotten. The Episcopal Church would continue on as if nothing of consequence had happened.

Why were appeals for reconciliation and unity successful not only in 1862 but also at the war's end? What prompted Episcopal leaders on all sides of the war to take such an irenic stand in the face of the horrors of the costliest American war, which led to the deaths of perhaps forty percent of all combatants and economic devastation in the South? Fear of schism and the desire to appear as moderate churchmen were evoked in official arguments, yet it is too glib to assert that these churchmen were simply following a traditional Anglican desire for compromise. Certainly there were close personal ties, social connections by class and education, and economic and business associations between Episcopal leaders in the North and South. The structure of the Episcopal Church, with its sensitivity to each bishop's diocesan sovereignty, also mitigated against taking controversial political stands. The bishop in his diocese could put forth an ecclesiastical version of a "states' rights" argument against the legislation of a federated church body.

In 1857, furthermore, a perceptive survey of religious opinion about slavery had noted that denominations with tight hierarchical polities tended to support the *status quo*, rather than notice political and social evils. As the leading Congregational pastor Henry Ward Beecher observed, some preachers (including Episcopalians) avoided the introduction of social themes like slavery, as it might hurt their credibility with business members of their congregations. Certainly many conservative Episcopalians believed that the church and its pulpits should not be "sullied by politics." This was particularly true in the South where, according to historian Gardiner Shattuck, a personal and "highly individualistic" faith prevailed which eschewed church's interference in social and political affairs. Avoidance of "purely political questions" was a habit of many Episcopal leaders throughout the nineteenth century. These and other reasons lay behind the Episcopal Church's official failure to deal with slavery as a political issue, let alone a moral one.[17]

Given the Episcopal Church's record during the Civil War, it is not surprising that the church's postwar ministry with African Americans and its support of newly freed citizens during Reconstruction were not successful. The 1865 General Convention linked its mission efforts to education and established a Freedman's Commission. (The 1868 Convention renamed this body as the "Commission on Home Missions to Colored People," no doubt to set it apart from the highly controversial federal Freedman's Bureau.) The commission was at first drawn into supplying immediate physical relief to destitute citizens; it then tried to establish high schools and colleges, most of which (with the exception of St. Augustine's College in North Carolina) did not survive beyond 1877. At this time the commission turned its strategies toward supporting Episcopal missions and missionaries. According to historian J. Carlton Hayden, the commission's "activities in the deep south were almost non-existent." The overall focus on education and mission was too little and too late. Throughout the South, predominately white churches lost most of their African-American members. As the learned African-American priest Alexander Crummell wrote, this exodus was hardly surprising:

> When freedom came the emancipated class, by one common impulse rushed from the chapels provided by their masters—deserted in multitudes the ministries of white preachers—in search for a ministry of their own race.[18]

General official reluctance in the Episcopal Church to name slavery as the cause of the war was mirrored by a continuing willingness, once war was over and emancipation had been declared, to let southerners deal in their own ways with the freed population. Friendships among the bishops and northern capitalists also favored rapid reconciliation in the South. General Sherman's promises of "Forty Acres and a Mule," which had created an explosion of hope in black communities, were soon abandoned under pressure from former property owners. The long record of Reconstruction's broken promises—including failed financial and educational institutions and return to a kind of rural serfdom that forced many newly freed citizens to sign contracts with their former masters—and the legacy of violence against blacks in all regions of the country was powerfully portrayed by the African-American intellectual W. E. B. Du Bois in *The Souls of Black Folk*, published in 1903.

While some southern bishops and other white clergy encouraged full membership and ministerial support for African-American Episcopalians, there were laity and clergy who wanted these church members to be segregated. Within the Episcopal Church there were repeated proposals to create a kind of racial apartheid in the church that in effect would have mirrored the secular Jim Crow legislation that gave legal force to white supremacy. Between 1874 and 1940 some southern leaders at General Conventions sought legislation authorizing racially demarcated "missionary districts." Crummell and his successors in black organizations and congregations, as well as some northern leaders, led the fight against making segregation a permanent feature of church life. While these measures for separate jurisdictions failed nationally, there were individual dioceses that denied African Americans and their congregations voting rights and participation at diocesan conventions, relegating them to different and separate structures for "their care."

A sorry record on race relations has been a component of Episcopal Church life since the Civil War. Until the 1960s, the Episcopal Church perpetuated its official silence on matters of race and racism, preferring to focus on educational issues and missionary concerns. This was the overall pattern for dealing with other "minorities," as documented by the church's response to Indian affairs. During the latter half of the nineteenth century, missionary and educational work proceeded amid official silence about the plight of the Native Americans and the government's wars against them.[19] The southern ethic of "strict noninterference of the churches in political affairs" would prove to be an expansive and "enduring legacy" beyond the Civil War years.[20]

The story of the Episcopal Church and the American Civil War provides a complex example of what happens when church leaders—in the interests of institutional unity and not rocking the boat—do not face directly into serious conflict. Some have applauded this instance of official ecclesiastical silence; others have rejoiced that there was no lasting ecclesiastical division in the church. Pleas for moderation and reconciliation are often popular and helpful. Yet, as the great American philosopher Thomas Paine once wrote, "Moderation in temper is always a virtue; moderation in principle is always a vice." A pointed example is found in Martin Luther King's 1963 "Letter from the Birmingham City Jail." Defending his participation in nonviolent protests, Dr. King expressed to white Alabama clerical leaders his grave disappointment with the "white moderate who is more devoted to 'order' than to justice." As W. E. B. Du Bois prophesied in 1903, "The problem of the twentieth century is the problem of the color-line."[21] The Episcopal Church in the Civil War had more than one opportunity to declare itself on the moral issue of human bondage. It did not speak, setting in place a legacy of denial that would long continue.

∾ Welcoming Conflict: The New Knowledge

Embracing difference and disagreement in consequential matters of faith is emphatically *not* an easy thing to do. We can empathize with those who, like Queen Elizabeth I, prefer to have things "settled" once and for all. What about faithful church members who, in the latter decades of the nineteenth century, experienced massive shifts in the wider culture occasioned by scientific developments about evolution and biblical studies that seemed to threaten their settled and cherished beliefs? Can we learn from their trials as we face our own? I hope so. There is much for us to learn from those who dealt directly with social questions of their time by drawing upon traditional theological resources.

During the late Victorian period (roughly the last third of the nineteenth century), there was a "crisis of faith" in England and America. Many believed that traditional religious truths were being undercut by new scientific discoveries. One of the meanings of the word "crisis" is "a turning point in progress," and they feared that, with the rise of new historical and scientific criticism from the 1860s onward, Christianity and progress would prove to be antithetical. Many Christians experienced considerable anxiety and fear about the impact of an increasingly scientific culture upon familiar religious beliefs. At the same time, a number of Anglican theologians and scientists waded into the new scientific terrains and eventually emerged with a deeper understandings of both theology and the universe.

Two main subjects attracted popular and learned attention. The first debate arose in response to scientific studies about evolution by Charles Darwin and others. Many people assumed that Darwin claimed that humanity was descended from the apes rather than created in the "image of God." Darwin's theories were caricatured together with those of the Positivists, who rejected theology in the light of positive facts:

> There was an ape in days that were earlier;
> Centuries passed and his hair became curlier;
> Centuries more and his thumb gave a twist,
> And he was man and a Positivist.[22]

Yet in his *Origin of Species* (1859) Darwin wrote only one modest sentence about humanity: "Light will be thrown on the origin of man and his history." While he later expanded upon this subject in *The Descent of Man* (1871), the idea of opposing theology was far from his mind. Darwin and other scientists who worked in such broad ranging fields as geology, biology, astronomy, economic theory, and the social sciences were actually engaged in an internal scientific debate. In effect, the work of the main evolutionists (with the exception of agnostics like the biologist T. H. Huxley) ended up replacing the natural theology of Isaac Newton with grander understandings of God's continuing presence in creation. Yet in the popular mind, debates about evolution loomed large. Would the supernatural truths of Christianity be able to withstand the challenges of scientific rationalism?

The second controversy was over the use of new scientific methods to study the Bible. Biblical or higher criticism meant investigating the Bible scientifically like any other historical document. It was pioneered in Germany by scholars who were reverent in spirit but asked pointedly direct questions about authorship, sources, literary forms, and the dating of texts in the Bible. Anglicans and other Christians worried about the conclusions and interpretations of these biblical scholars. What if traditional beliefs, including a belief in the miraculous, were directly contradicted by these modern rationalists? Were such beliefs now to be considered old-fashioned? What if Moses did not write the Pentateuch? Could biblical accounts of creation in Genesis be incorrect? If so, what did this say about the omnipotence of God? The questions, fears, and anxieties raised by higher criticism were considerable for Anglicans on both sides of the Atlantic.

A variety of Anglican responses to the challenges of scientific and historical criticism emerged. The most significant of these appeared in 1889 as a series of essays edited by Charles Gore and entitled *Lux Mundi: A Series of Studies in the Religion of the Incarnation*. The Latin phrase here means "light of the world." It refers aptly to the doctrine of the Incarnation as the light by which these essayists illumined and addressed the "crisis of faith" questions of their day. The authors drew upon the central theological resource of the Incarnation to discover new moral and intellectual insights. Charles Gore's preface states *Lux Mundi*'s approach to knowledge:

> The real development of theology is...the process in which the church, standing firm in her old truths, enters into the apprehension of the new social and intellectual movements of each age: and because "the truth makes her free," is able to assimilate all new material, to welcome and give its place to all new knowledge, to throw herself into the sanctification of each new social order, bringing forth out of her treasures things new and old, and showing again and again her power for witnessing under changed conditions to the catholic capacity of her faith and life.

With this declaration, the *Lux Mundi* authors boldly shaped a method that invited modern Anglicans to welcome new knowledge as an ally rather than an enemy of catholic, incarnational Christianity. These theologians envisioned an immanent God at work in all of creation: in humanity, in nature, in art, in science, and in social progress.[23]

The essayists of *Lux Mundi* wished to provide genuine contact between people of faith and critical scientific studies, and helped many in late Victorian culture recognize the compatibility of religion and science. Aubrey Moore and J. R. Illingworth, in particular, welcomed evolution and similar critical discoveries as helpful "new ways of looking at things." Moore presented evolution as restoring "the truth of divine immanence." Such knowledge, the essayists conclude, enhances (rather than contradicts) the wonders of divine creation. To these and other challenges Gore would later directly respond: "In the broadest sense 'the Bible was not given to teach us science,' and does in fact speak only in terms of the science of its times." In time, both liberal and conservative Anglicans held positive attitudes toward science. The Anglo-Catholic leader Edward Bouverie Pusey, for example, eventually acknowledged the truth of evolution provided (as he once remarked) it did not entail "belief in our apedom."[24]

In *Lux Mundi* Charles Gore directly affirms the value of biblical criticism. In his essay on "The Holy Spirit and Inspiration," Gore emphasizes that inspired guidance of the Holy Spirit allows the church to interpret scripture faithfully. "Christianity brings with it a doctrine of the inspiration of Holy Scripture, but is not based upon it." While Gore acknowledges that these new methods challenged contemporaries to make "considerable changes" in their conceptions of scripture, he pointedly notes that these changes were "no greater" than those involved in accepting heliocentric astronomy. Writing from the perspective of a faithful inquirer after truth, Gore argues that the conclusions of critical scholarship should be welcomed:

> There [does not] appear to be any real danger that the criticism of the Old Testament will ultimately diminish our reverence for it. In the case of the New Testament certainly we are justified in feeling that modern investigation has resulted in immensely augmenting our understanding of the different books and has distinctly fortified and enriched our sense of their inspiration.[25]

Gore's overall plea was that theologians leave the field of biblical studies open for reasonable and free discussion. Not surprisingly, his essay in *Lux Mundi* initially attracted hostility; there were some who feared that this brilliant young theologian had capitulated to German rationalism.

However, over the following decades, the approach of Gore and the other *Lux Mundi* authors would eventually prove successful in helping Anglicans accept new methods of biblical study and new scientific developments. The teaching of higher criticism gradually gained ground in England and in American Episcopal seminaries following the lead of the Episcopal Theological School in Cambridge, Massachusetts. By 1899, both the Lambeth Conference of Anglican Bishops and the Episcopal House of Bishops had affirmed critical historical study of the Bible. Although the acceptance of these new ideas by the general public has taken more time, and debates about biblical interpretation continue to this day, Anglicans have tended to welcome, learn from, and engage modern biblical scholarship.

The strength of the English intellectual tradition, heralded by Thomas Cranmer, John Jewel, and Richard Hooker, prevailed in later centuries. Anglicans came to embrace the other cultural and intellectual challenges raised by modern critical teaching, including the pressing social questions of their time. For Anglicans, the emphasis of the *Lux Mundi* authors on progressive disclosure and understanding would prove beneficial in a variety of debates. Their legacy not only provides a helpful bridge into the twentieth century, it also presents us with an essential key for living with disagreement in a new millennium.

This successful tradition of intellectual openmindedness may also prove beneficial to contemporary Episcopalians in our encounters with today's rapid pace of scientific and technological change. How fast is our knowledge changing? Vartan Gregorian, former president of the New York Public Library, has observed that the available information doubles every five years. It is no wonder that questions persist about the character of Christian belief in this age of new scientific discoveries.

Today's contemporary challenges have attracted some of the best minds in the Anglican Communion. For example, Episcopal biblical scholar Frederick Borsch has outlined the huge shifts in scientific understandings that have occurred since Darwin: from Newtonian science to relativity, and on to quantum theory and chaos theory. He points to complex evidence suggesting that creativity in every form and organization "takes place at the edges of order and chaos." Concluding not with a question about God's absence or with fear about what the insights of science can portend, but with a belief that God is still in the process of creating, he writes,

> There are... enormous opportunities for those who believe that their faith in God and the forms of truth which science can discover should not be in conflict. What may be most important for this integration is a profound awareness that God is so present and intimate to all that is that we might even speak of the world as God's body.[26]

Bishop Borsch, like his *Lux Mundi* forebears, envisions God's abiding and incarnate presence in the universe.

Similarly, I have found the writings of John Polkinghorne, a theoretical physicist and Anglican priest, extremely helpful in exploring contemporary debates about science and religion. Although I am an eager reader, usually I do not turn to texts about science; indeed, my scientific literacy has not been extended since high school days. Yet Polkinghorne has inspired me to learn more about the world of quarks and gluons, "systems that are at least a hundred million times smaller than atoms." Not only does he introduce readers to the new sciences of quantum and chaos theory, but explores how the disciplines of science and religion are "intellectual cousins" in their pursuit of "motivated belief." Polkinghorne suggests that "science is concerned with answering the question *How?* And theology is concerned with answering the question *Why?*" As constructive theologians, both Borsch and Polkinghorne resemble the authors of *Lux Mundi*, writing a hundred years later. They also envision a universe that is incarnationally open to human and divine agency. Polkinghorne concludes: "God is as much the Creator today as God was fifteen billion years ago."[27]

These are hopeful words on which to end a chapter about living with conflict. When serious divisions occur, our theological ancestors have taught us the consequences of avoiding controversy, and the benefits of dealing openly with conflict and embracing new understandings. They have left us testimonies from times in which they affirmed the value of different and opposing opinions and yet remained in communion with one another. Through their experience, we can discern lessons about the inevitability of change in the church and about the dangers of seeking unity at all costs. Theologically they have encouraged us to illumine difficult challenges with a bright theological light, the "light of the world." Making sense of the richness of our world has involved Anglicans and other Christians in drawing upon the mysteries of divine revelation, as well as delving into mysterious new sciences. Perhaps this historical and theological tradition can also help us address our own pressing crises. This promise is one we can carry forward into a new chapter, as we consider what history might have to teach us about caring for the environment in which we live.

Chapter Five

Recycling Tradition

Traditional parish customs from the Church of England contain many curiosities, among them the custom of "walking the bounds." This is a ritual procession of clergy and people walking round the local boundaries of the whole geographical parish, not just the church building. In this procession the congregation invites God's blessing with psalms and prayers for the earth, harvest, crops, herds, and other living things gathered therein. This marking of local geographical boundaries, which occurred one to three times a year, depending on local custom, was also intended to encourage neighborliness, extend charity, seek reconciliation of differences, and promote greater understanding among those living in close proximity. Above all, this custom emphasized the close relationship between the parish community and the land. George Herbert, the author of a seventeenth-century guide to parish life, *The Country Parson*, observed that in walking the bounds there is much "friendliness."

A remnant of this yearly tradition so loved by our English country ancestors has been "recycled" for us in the Episcopal Church in the form of rogation days, which are found in the *Book of Common Prayer.* "Rogation" comes from the Latin word for petition, or intercession. In early pagan and Christian observances, rogation came to be associated with processions to the fields to pray for the flourishing of the crops. Such occasions were also marked by the voluntary restraints of fasting and abstinence. Although these observances were not mentioned in the early sixteenth-century prayer books, Queen Elizabeth I highly favored these processions and in 1559 ordered that they be regularly observed. Eventually rogation days were included in the 1662 prayer book, which is still in use today. I like to think of rogation observances as the predecessors of today's Earth Day celebrations, which were first established in 1970. George Herbert's advice still prevails: such observances can encourage friendliness and charity among neighbors who share in their dependence upon earth's resources.

Let me offer one illustration. Once in the 1960s as part of an inner-city, south-side Chicago parish, I joined others as we "walked the bounds" of our neighborhood on a Saturday morning. We were a straggling (and struggling) congregation, singing songs as we were led in a candlelit yet jazzy procession by towering teenage acolytes, one a basketball player and the other a local gang member. As we walked, we became more neighborly among ourselves *and* we met many of our neighbors. Some of these newfound neighbors accepted the invitation to join us back at the parish hall for sandwiches. A few weeks later the senior warden, an economics professor, led us in learning more about the demographic composition and material needs of our parish's neighborhood. The 1960s was a time of widespread violence in many cities, a period when it was increasingly advantageous for inner-city parishes to know the neighborhood and its leaders. Friendliness and communication about material needs in this fragile social environment were lifelines for survival, respect, and mutual support.

Today few of us live in the pastoral surroundings of George Herbert's seventeenth-century parishioners, nor do most parishes define themselves by geographical boundaries. Church members travel from nearby and far away to worship in a particular church building. Typically there are members of many religious faiths living in the same geographical area, and several places of worship are often found in the same neighborhood. If we walked about our neighborhoods today we might well find that the overall environment in which we live and form religious communities is increasingly burdened. Some parishes are situated in prosperous locales while others are not, yet all geographical areas are subject to the limitations of earth's bounty and the deepening ecological crisis that now faces what the prayer book calls "this fragile earth, our island home" (BCP 370). If our Reformation ancestors originally understood their responsibility to include care for the well-being of a geographical region, then what is our environmental legacy as Christians and Anglicans today?

There are few among us who, in the past twenty years, have not developed a new or renewed awareness of the depletion of earth's resources due to human use and misuse. Most of us are increasingly aware of creation's fragility as arable land and verdant forests are decimated and fresh air and clean water are polluted by human use. The variety and longevity of all species are under assault, as the loss of healthy habitats inevitably leads to the extinction of many forms of life; one conservative estimate speaks of ten thousand species destroyed in a year. Also, the human toll taken by environmental devastation must not be underestimated. While we are all affected, poorer populations throughout the world are the most vulnerable, especially those who live in places of destitution, hunger, and persistent cycles of famine and disease. How much more can our ecosystem tolerate? The Worldwatch Institute estimated in 1990 that we have about forty years to reverse pollution and energy depletion patterns that threaten life on this planet.[1]

None of these crises can be considered in isolation, since our new scientific understandings testify to the interrelatedness of all reality. Today's scientists describe a cosmos whose elements are constantly interacting and changing in ways that are not yet fully understood. We inhabit a globe that is multiform, complex, and mysterious. Accordingly, no one single cause of the ecological crisis can be identified at the expense of others. Overpopulation among people who are impoverished certainly plays a role, as does our devotion to expectations of unlimited industrial growth and unrestricted consumerism. Anglican bishop David Jenkins asks pointedly, "Are we ready to have...a society where being a neighbor is valued at least as highly as being a consumer?"[2]

In this chapter I want to explore the role of tradition in helping us address pressing new issues by focusing on the spiritual dimensions of today's ecological crisis. Can a deepened understanding of resources from church history prove helpful in this matter? What role can tradition play in facing dangers unknown to our ancestors? In short, how can history help us look forward? What we can learn from history about living faithfully and responsibly in a world beset by environmental problems? How are Christians, whose eyes are often focused on heaven, to come to terms with the material world? Are there distinctive Anglican resources that might prove helpful? For *what* we do about the environment compels us to rethink *who* we are in the cosmic order and how we are related to God and to one another.

∿ **Recycling Theology**

"Recycling" may become as important a word for twenty-first-century Christians as "reformation" was to our sixteenth-century forebears. This apt image blending an ecological activity with history and theology was first suggested by Kwok Pui Lan, an Anglican theologian originally from Hong Kong. She points out that the idea of "recycling Christianity" is not new: it is anticipated in such traditional concepts as "conversion, *metanoia*, and even resurrection."[3] Each of these theological concepts is a religious way of speaking about change. Conversion refers to the adoption of a new religious belief, *metanoia* is a Greek word meaning the repeated pattern of "turning around" to envision truth anew, and resurrection involves moving from death to new life in Christ. The concept of recycling also implies preserving what is of value in a familiar object to use it again in the future, perhaps in a new and surprising way. The practice of recycling helps integrate our lives by valuing all matter—human as well as animal, vegetable, and mineral resources—and by caring for all of earth's elemental properties. Some of our traditional beliefs would benefit from a recycling process as well, allowing them to be reappropriated for wiser use.

The image of recycling also provides us with a helpful way to think about the recovery of central theological traditions. Recycling is like reformation: it rediscovers the valuable core of a tradition and, once it has been simplified and the centuries of unnecessary accretions removed, it can be put to use for future generations. Reformation and recycling alike reflect faith in an abiding yet surprising God who comes among us to "do a new thing" (Isaiah 43:19).

The modern ecological movement testifies to our need to reform past habits, to seek new strategies, and to recycle valuable resources.

There are a number of cultures and religions that have valuable contributions to make to environmental theology. Many of the spiritual practices and beliefs of Native American peoples, for example, are richly grounded in ecological wisdom. Aboriginal peoples throughout the world express ways of knowing and relating to the created order that will again be important if we are to sustain a high quality of life on earth.

On the other hand, some commentators have boldly blamed Christian theologians for the environmental crisis, because of their emphasis on humanity's dominion over nature, based on the first chapters of Genesis.[4] In addition, Christians have tended to value spiritual and otherworldly aspirations over the material realities of life. This tendency is a healthy corrective to greed and overconsumption, but it goes too far when we assume that life on earth is literally "immaterial" to spiritual health. Christian theology is not in fact uniformly dismissive of nature. On the contrary, I discern within traditional Anglicanism some positive elements derived from early Christian and medieval theology that affirm the sacred character of the natural world.

~ Let Us Sing to the Lord!

One fine way to discover and "recycle" our tradition's full range of teaching on creation is to read the daily office. Morning Prayer provides for regular recitation of psalms and canticles glorifying God for the universe, earth, and all living creatures. It is of course possible (as many do) to read the morning office privately, day by day. Yet, for me, there is a different character to praying the morning office with others. In fact, I grew up in a parish where Morning Prayer was the principal Sunday service and Holy Communion was celebrated only one Sunday a month. Today the reverse tends to be true, so that many Episcopalians, especially newcomers to this denomination, may not know what they have missed in the morning office. I was raised in the worshipful presence of a God whose ways were "known upon earth," a God who, according to the canticle called the *Venite*, held together all "the caverns of the earth," including the hills, the seas, and the dry lands. Acknowledging God's love of creation has long been an essential part of traditional Anglican worship.

As our historical theology has developed since the sixteenth and seventeenth centuries and as it has drawn upon earlier theological traditions, it tends to envision the goodness of God's created order as a spiritual and material whole. This distinct tradition offers us valuable help in developing a healthy theological perspective on the environment. In this section I will proceed first by looking selectively at treasured sources in early eastern and medieval Christianity and next at the Reformation theologian Richard Hooker, who will provide us with a significant resource for Anglican teaching about creation. Hooker's assessments illumine early Anglican understandings of sacramental theology, which underscore God's love of all things. This sympathetic perspective about life on earth has been apparent in Anglican thinking and worship since at least the end of the sixteenth century.

Our Reformation ancestors often drew upon earlier theologians, adopting many theological viewpoints from the Christian east—the Christianity of Basil the Great, Gregory of Nyssa, and Gregory of Nazianzus. Greek and Syrian theologians tended to view matter as a sacred part of God's creation and so emphasized humanity's responsibilities toward the created order. In this they were very different from writers of the Christian west, who tended to focus on human sinfulness and the evil inherent in material creation. In the west ideas of salvation came to be envisioned narrowly rather than cosmically, with little that was positive to say about humanity's place in nature. This individualistic focus of redemption was adopted by Roman Catholicism and later emphasized within most of the Protestant churches that grew out of the Continental Reformation. It is the basis for the sociologist Max Weber's description of Protestants' "disenchantment with the world."

In the eastern church, however, Gregory of Nyssa and Basil the Great saw creation itself as a mirror of the Creator's glory and reveled in the divine wonder that filled "the stars, planets, comets," and even the abyss. Their compatriot, Gregory of Nazianzus, similarly extolled the earth for revealing God's word and wisdom. "Study fish," he once advised:

> In the water they fly, and they find the air they need in the water. They would die in our atmosphere, just as we would die in the water. Watch their habits, their way of mating and procreating their kind, their beauty, their permanent homes and their wanderings.[5]

Gregory of Nazianzus also looked at bees and spiders, wondering at the source of their ingenuity and love of work. Could it be other than God? These early Christian monastics and theologians were not only interested in the world of nature. Many of them enjoyed studying such subjects as cosmology, astronomy, botany, horticulture, zoology, and human anatomy.

Another decisive influence of the eastern church on Anglican thinking about creation was that of Isaac the Syrian, a seventh-century monk and author of ascetical texts focusing on Christian perfection. In the passage that follows, Isaac describes a charitable heart and directly connects a love of creation with the gift of compassion.

> It is a heart which is burning with charity for the whole of creation, for men, for the birds, for the beasts, for the demons—for all creatures. He who has such a heart cannot see or call to mind a creature without his eyes being filled with tears by reason of the immense compassion which seizes his heart; a heart which is softened and can no longer bear to see or learn from others of any suffering, even the smallest pain, being inflicted upon a creature.

Thus the interrelationship of humanity with all creatures was central to the divine order. Indeed, Gregory of Nyssa envisioned humanity as a mediator linking the spiritual and material worlds in praise of God. Notwithstanding the reality of sin, humanity and nature alike essentially reflect the goodness of God's creation.[6]

Basil the Great, Gregory of Nyssa, and Gregory of Nazianzus are included as saints in the Episcopal Church's calendar of lesser feasts and fasts, but we also see their historical legacies in Eucharistic Prayer D found in the 1979 *Book of Common Prayer:*

> Fountain of life and source of all goodness, you made all things and fill them with your blessing; you created them to rejoice in the splendor of your radiance. (BCP 373)

Similarly, a hymn by John of Damascus, "The day of resurrection," proclaims the glorious unity of creation that is revealed in the resurrection:

Now let the heavens be joyful
    let earth her song begin,
the round world keep high triumph,
    and all that is therein;
let all things seen and unseen
    their notes together blend,
for Christ the Lord is risen,
    our joy that hath no end.[7]

In these and other citations drawn from the spirituality of the eastern fathers, all of nature expresses the divine ordering of creation.

Many of us, of course, have also heard of two western medieval saints whose lives are celebrated in the Christian calendar: Benedict of Nursia and Francis of Assisi. Among the western divines, these two religious leaders were most distinctly attentive to God's presence throughout the natural world. Benedict, whose life spanned the fifth and sixth centuries and included a long period in a hermitage, expresses the recurrent pattern of renunciation and affirmation so characteristic of monastic life. For example, a monk withdraws to the relative isolation of the desert and then returns to offer praise to God for all of creation. Furthermore, the Benedictine Rule, with its emphasis on stability—long-term living in a particular community— involves relating with responsible care to the cycles of nature. Benedict's Rule has another significance for Anglicans, too, since its ordering of daily prayer, the Divine Office, would later figure in Thomas Cranmer's sixteenth-century liturgical reconstruction of the offices for Morning and Evening Prayer. In my imagination, I often hear Benedict's imperative in his prologue to the Rule: "Listen!" as I begin to pray the morning office.

Francis of Assisi has become for many in recent years the patron saint of ecologists. Although his image has been highly sentimentalized, Francis preached and practiced a radical message of simplicity, restraint, and love for creation; Evelyn Underhill described him as a spiritual revolutionary. When we celebrate his feast day by hosting a blessing of domestic animals, our efforts are at best tame (if sometimes noisy) echoes of Francis' profound insight that humanity cannot be considered separately from the rest of the cosmos. He emphasized that practicing the virtue of humility would lead us to abandon aggression toward the rest of nature, and his "Canticle of the Sun" concludes: "Let creatures all give thanks to thee, and serve in great humility." Both Franciscan reverence for creation and Benedictine stewardship of the environment provide important historical testimonies that can help us connect spiritual health with the well-being of creation.[8]

With today's growing interest in the environment, church historians are identifying other figures who have emphasized the need to cherish and sustain the natural world. One of these is Hildegard of Bingen, a twelfth-century Benedictine abbess, theologian, poet, scientist, musician, and composer whose mystical visions underscore the unity and goodness of creation. Another figure loved by Anglicans is Julian of Norwich. Her revelations of God's love were often expressed through the goodness of creation: in the hazelnut she saw the blessed microcosm of "all that is," and she spoke of God as a father *and* a mother, one who loves us in creation. Like Francis, Julian drew ethical conclusions from these earthly connections. She taught that all who have "general love for all [their] fellow Christians in God have love toward everything that is."[9]

Benedict, Hildegard, Francis, and Julian are part of a deep vein in western Christian thought emphasizing the goodness of the physical world and God's loving relationship to the whole of creation. By insisting that the natural world was the good creation of a loving God, these medieval monastics and visionaries challenged the bias against nature in much of western Christian thought. It remained for Richard Hooker, the most influential Reformation theologian in England, to draw these early Christian and medieval insights into a truly Anglican theology of creation.

~ The Glorious Works of Nature

In his *Laws of Ecclesiastical Polity*, a vast theological defense of the Reformation in England, Hooker emphatically proclaimed God's goodness in creation. More important still, he gave Anglicans who came after him some specific theological arguments illustrating how the church and its members participate in the work of God's ongoing creation. Hooker set about this, first of all, by telling us that nature itself gives us our knowledge of God. The foundation for natural law is planted by God in creation and all civic laws are derived from this base. Anglicans are used to thinking of scripture, tradition, and reason as the three authoritative sources of doctrine. Hooker himself lays out this approach in the *Laws*. However, he then goes on to describe how God speaks to us in a *variety* of ways:

> As [wisdom's] ways are of sundry kinds, so her manner of teaching is not merely one and the same. Some things she openeth by the sacred books of Scripture; some things by the glorious works of nature: with some things she inspireth them only from above by spiritual influence, in some things she leadeth and traineth them only by worldly experience and practice.[10]

The "glorious works of nature" and "worldly experience" are analogous to "the sacred books of scripture": they are *living* books that lead us to know God anew. Hooker's broad view of knowledge set him apart from other Reformation theologians, who saw only the Bible as authoritative. His appreciation of the wisdom that fills the world and our own experience of it, and his openness to many different sources of knowledge—material and spiritual, biblical and traditional, reasoned and inspired—are essential today for ecologists, empirical scientists, professional theologians, and everyday believers. We are free to imagine and learn about life on Mars as well as on Earth.

Another critical feature of Hooker's thought is his belief that God's influence is found throughout creation, including humanity itself:

> God hath his influence into the very essence of all things....All things are therefore partakers of God, they are his offspring, his influence is in them, and the personal wisdom of God is for that very cause said to excel in nimbleness or agility, to pierce into all intellectual, pure, and subtle spirits, to go through all, and to reach unto everything which is.[11]

If this is true, then the God who made animate and inanimate things in the beginning also continues to hold and influence life from within. This leads us directly to the Incarnation, Hooker says, which is still another way that matter—in this case human flesh—reveals the mind of God. The *Book of Common Prayer*'s collect for the Incarnation speaks of a God "who wonderfully created, and yet more wonderfully restored, the dignity of human nature" (BCP 252). In other words, God's willingness to take on human flesh not only improved the quality of human nature, it also moved us further toward God's purposes. Like the eastern theologians Basil and Gregory, Hooker envisions matter as a positive, not a negative: it is the medium of the Spirit.

For us the most significant feature of Hooker's theology of creation is the fact that he sees the whole world, infused as it is with divine goodness, as intimately connected and interdependent. If God dwells in "the very essence of all things," then

> God hath created nothing simply for itself: but each thing in all things, and of everything each part in other have such interest, that in the whole world nothing is found whereunto any thing created can say, "I need thee not."[12]

For it is human pride, not divine intent, that separates us from one another and from the goodness of creation. We are all related; we are all complementary. A. M. Allchin suggests that this view of everything as potentially sacramental is distinctive to Reformation thought. While other theologians tended to oppose grace and nature, divine and human, the church and the Bible, "the Anglican tradition has tried always to proceed by way of both/and, holding together things apparently opposed."[13] Delight in the physical universe is inseparable from delight in God's spiritual gifts. Thus today, when the *Book of Common Prayer* bids worshipers to pray for "Christ's Church *and* the world," the overall framework is one of coherence and not of separate spheres.

At the same time, a distinction must be made here between *pantheism*—the belief that God and the universe are identical—and *panentheism*, the belief that while God's influence is in all things, God still transcends all things. This distinction is important: Christian appreciation of God's presence in nature is not the same thing as nature worship. For Anglicans the focus of our theology and our worship is a God whose presence extends throughout creation *and* beyond our wildest imaginings of this world. Whether we are "studying fish," honoring the goodness of creation, or joining together in the sacraments, it is an Anglican expectation that our sense of the transcendent wonder, ingenuity, and mystery of God will be lovingly revealed.

∾ Infused with Divinity

I mentioned in an earlier chapter that one of my favorite definitions of spirituality is "theology walking." By this I mean theology that is accessible enough to be helpfully put to work in our daily lives. Even though I am a fan of Richard Hooker's theology, I have to admit that his style and comprehensiveness make everyday use difficult at best. Where else can we locate spiritual resources that are more accessible and yet (like Hooker) deeply grounded in cherishing and sustaining life on earth?

As a child, much of the theology I learned came from singing hymns. Perhaps the same is true of children—and adults—today: hymns can provide rich theological and ecological resources. *The Hymnal 1982* of the Episcopal Church, like the revised hymnals of other faith traditions, has expanded its imagery to include a larger, more diverse repertoire. One of my cherished childhood hymns was "All things bright and beautiful, all creatures great and small," pointing sweetly to "each little flower that opens, each little bird that sings," but today's children can find less sentimental, more robust images. For example, the hymn text for "Earth and all stars" includes references to "loud rushing planets," "loud pounding hammers," "loud boiling test tubes," and even "loud sounding wisdom." Even more robust is Catherine Cameron's contemporary text, "God, who stretched the spangled heavens." Cameron evokes humanity's newfound abilities for space travel and atomic power, noting as well the possibility of "life's destruction." She points directly to our reliance on divine guidance:

> God, who stretched the spangled heavens
>   infinite in time and place,
> flung the suns in burning radiance
>   through the silent fields of space:
> we, your children in your likeness,
>   share inventive powers with you:
> Great Creator, still creating,
>   show us what we yet may do.[14]

"All things bright and beautiful" is a fine place to begin, yet as Cameron suggests there may be more that God calls us to take on in the future. Hymns can make theology more accessible but also challenge us to look at our assumptions about faithfulness.

Another valuable resource for Anglicans and other Christians seeking a spirituality grounded in creation is seventeenth-century English religious literature. It is a period that produced a remarkable flowering of talent: a creative group of preachers, poets, parish priests, and bishops who have been referred to collectively as the Caroline divines because they lived and wrote during the reigns of Charles I and Charles II. These theologians and poets celebrated the world that Hooker described as "infused with divinity," where both humanity and nature are joined in the praise of God. Their collective spiritual heritage was grounded in communal worship and personal devotion, and expressed in the moral character of daily life.

It is odd that this harmonious spiritual legacy, which stresses the complementarity of all elements in God's universe, comes to us from a century that was marked by severe religious and political turbulence both in England and throughout Europe. In England these divisions led to the executions of the Archbishop of Canterbury, William Laud, in 1645 and King Charles I in 1649, the disestablishment of the Church of England as the religion of the realm, and a chaotic civil war. One English historian has described this period of "no Bishop and no King" as a time when "the world was turned upside down." Marked by change, disruption, and an explosion of new knowledge, the seventeenth century had a need for religious truth that would not evade the marked complexity of daily living. If the sixteenth century was the period when the worship, polity, and theology of the reformed church in England were established, then the seventeenth century was the time when Anglicanism produced a rich flowering of devotional literature. By the end of the century the monarchy was secured with the restoration of Charles II in 1660 and the Church of England was established within the context of a religiously pluralistic society. Anglican theology grew to express itself as a moral way of life.

Among the Caroline divines I will focus on three seventeenth-century Anglican clergy—Lancelot Andrewes, George Herbert, and Thomas Traherne. There are others I could mention, of course, including John Donne and Jeremy Taylor, but these three best represent a rich and enduring strain within Anglican spirituality. Theirs is a legacy of theology, preaching, and poetry that repeatedly praises the unified and sacred character of creation. This historical period, perhaps more than any other, grounds Anglican thought in the goodness of the whole of physical creation and the sanctity of this world.

Lancelot Andrewes

If I had to choose only one divine from this period it would be Lancelot Andrewes, for Andrewes profoundly influenced the shaping of Anglican spirituality. We might describe him as having three successful careers. First, he was a hardworking and distinguished biblical scholar who knew fifteen languages. We continue to be the beneficiaries of his scholarship, in that Andrewes was one of the translators of the Authorized (King James)Version of the Bible. Second, he was the most famous preacher of his day, leaving ninety-six sermons in print, nineteen of them on prayer and the Lord's Prayer. T. S. Eliot would later laud Andrewes as an artful preacher who "takes a word and derives a world from it." Finally, Andrewes was a bishop, a man of prayer who was warmly liked by his contemporaries at a time when most bishops were not highly esteemed. His own source book of notes and reflections on prayer, entitled *Preces Privatae* (or *Private Devotions*), was published after his death. Andrewes had a rich capacity for intimate friendship with God and with his neighbors, and his prayers are a window into the corporate and personal dimensions of prayer.[15]

Three achievements in particular of this Anglican divine can help us build a responsible environmental spirituality. Andrewes envisions prayer as consistently inclusive and generously expansive. Prayer is "an interpreter of hope" for all people. In his *Private Devotions*, Andrewes shapes petitions for all: for the whole human family, for the whole church (the churches of east and west, of Rome and of the Reformation), and for all believers, including non-Christians. He believed that, whether we pray in public or in private, by ourselves or with others, we never pray alone. He advises that even on those occasions when our prayers are "faint," this weakness is overcome by the "fervent" prayers of others. Andrewes' broad awareness of the catholicity of Christian belief and prayer allowed him to assert a fundamental understanding of the boundaries that Anglicans share with others: "One canon..., two testaments, three creeds, four general councils, five centuries and the series of Fathers in that period." Generations of students have found this a helpful way to summarize historic Anglican boundaries of faith.[16]

As Andrewes invites prayer for the whole of humanity, so too he grounds prayer within the context of the whole of creation. His understanding of prayer in the *Private Devotions* and in his sermons on Genesis is set within a universe perfected by God's grace. He begins the week, for example, with this daily intercession: "Let us beseech the Lord for the whole creation; a supply of seasons, healthful, fruitful and peaceful." It is not surprising that Andrewes was a student of nature. As his biographer reports, he delighted in "grass, herbs, corn, trees, cattle, earth, waters, heavens, any of the creatures." Andrewes contemplated nature for theological and moral reasons. Like the eastern fathers, he sought through nature to study the mind of God and the responsibility of humanity. Andrewes' interests resemble the habits of subsequent Anglican clergy who have delighted in studying the natural sciences as well as theology.[17]

For Andrewes, this foundation of a life of corporate and personal prayer reaching out to the whole of creation was not an object to be admired or privately hoarded. The moral character of the Christian life was at the heart of his preaching. The contemplative life invites us into the active life. He criticizes those who passively "lie still,...laying all upon Christ's shoulders." Faith, for Andrewes, "inspires effort." In a passage from the *Private Devotions* he draws upon biblical language to express ways of seeking God's guidance:

> In every imagination of our heart:
>   the words of our lips:

the works of our hands:
the ways of our feet.[18]

Clearly this holy man invokes a spirituality that "walks" as well as prays. For Andrewes and his contemporaries, theology took shape in an active and prayerful life.

George Herbert

One of the promising younger scholars that Andrewes befriended was George Herbert, whom we first met at the start of this chapter. In addition to *The Country Parson*, some of us may also know Herbert as the author of three poetic texts set to music in *The Hymnal 1982*. This time we turn to Herbert primarily as a poet, to deepen our appreciation of creation in seventeenth-century spirituality and devotion.

Herbert, like Andrewes, was prodigiously learned. His active ordained ministry, however, was less than three years in length. His service to the church concluded not as a bishop but as the rector of a small country parish. During Herbert's short life he was a friend of Andrewes, of the noted preacher and poet John Donne, and of Nicholas Ferrar, founder of a religious community at Little Gidding. After his death Herbert's popularity grew enormously, largely due to the posthumous publication of his book of religious poems, *The Temple*. This small volume of verse went through eight editions from Herbert's death in 1633 to the restoration of the monarchy with Charles II in 1660. Devoted readers of Herbert included Charles I, one of Oliver Cromwell's chaplains, royalists throughout the century, and a number of other nonconformist leaders. One edition of *The Temple* included a concordance so that preachers "of any persuasion" could easily refer to Herbert, much as they did to the scriptures. In a time of schism and religious divisions, Herbert's poetry inspired many believers. The noted

Puritan Richard Baxter, although not partial to Anglicans, aptly summarized the quality of Herbert's voice:

> Herbert speaketh to God like one who really believeth God, and whose business in the world is most *with God.* Heart-work and Heaven-work make up his book.[19]

Herbert shared many of the theological emphases of his near contemporaries, Hooker and Andrewes, displaying their devotional themes in poetry. The sacramentality of creation, indeed of all God's providence, includes "sponges, nonsense and sense; mines, th' earth and plants." "Each thing that is," he continues, "hath many ways in store to honor thee." Like Hooker, Herbert envisions God's presence in all things. This is cause for abundant praise, as Herbert proclaims in "Antiphon":

> Let all the world in ev'ry corner sing,
>   *My God and King.*
>
> The heav'ns are not too high,
> His praise may thither fly:
> The earth is not too low,
> His praises there may grow.
>
> Let all the world in ev'ry corner sing,
>   *My God and King.*

Here again is the familiar emphasis on the divine character of the universe. With consummate care and insight Herbert directly connects creation with preservation. He writes in *The Country Parson*:

> For Nature, [the Parson] sees not how a house could be either built without a builder, or kept in repair without a housekeeper.... For Preservation is a creation; and more, it is continued Creation.

It is worth pausing for a moment on Herbert's reflection that preservation is "continued creation." What a strong ecological mandate he sends us from the midst of the seventeenth century.[20]

In grace-filled poetry Herbert evokes two other themes that Andrewes favored. Prayer is the foundation for a life of faith. Both *The Temple* and *The Country Parson* present common prayer as grounding the work of the church and her people. Again, the prayers of the gathered community surpass the valuable practice of private devotion:

> Though private prayer be a brave design,
> Yet public hath more promises, more love.

Herbert's wonder at the power of prayer is best heard in his sonnet "Prayer":

> Prayer the Church's banquet, Angels' age,
>   God's breath in man returning to his birth,
>   The soul in paraphrase, heart in pilgrimage
> The Christian plummet sounding heav'n and earth. . . .
>
> Softness, and peace, and joy, and love, and bliss,
>   Exalted Manna, gladness of the best,
>   Heaven in ordinary, man well drest,
> The milky way, the bird of Paradise,
>
> Church-bells beyond the stars heard, the soul's blood,
> The land of spices; something understood.[21]

Today when new students and old friends ask me about the efficacy of prayer, it is Herbert's "something understood" that often comes to mind.

Like other Caroline divines, Herbert underscored the practical and moral aspects of an active life of faith. No act is too small to be of worth. In "Elixir," with its allusion to turning base metals into gold, Herbert invites us to value everyday practices as offerings to God:

Teach me, my God and King,
In all things thee to see,
And what I do in any thing,
To do it as for thee.[22]

One scholar of Anglican moral theology has called this poem the "best known poetical example" of translating theory into practice.[23] Herbert's emphasis on everyday expressions of faithfulness anticipates Jeremy Taylor's invitation to "Holy Living" and "Holy Dying." It is important to recall that the efforts by the Caroline divines to frame a broad, unified understanding of spirituality were offered within a societal context of turmoil and division. Their spirituality invites engagement in the world without evading its complexity. This rich testimony of praise to God was to be sung "in ev'ry corner."[24]

Thomas Traherne

I wish to draw my reflections on the Caroline divines to a close by introducing the third, lesser known member of the trio, Thomas Traherne. Unlike Andrewes and Herbert, this Anglican poet, priest, and mystic is not included on the Episcopal calendar of saints; like Herbert, Traherne's life was short and most of his poetry and prose was published after his death. Traherne's fourteen years of ordained service included a small parish in Hereford, a chaplaincy in London, and spiritual guidance to his patrons during the early years of the Restoration. He is known as one of the seventeenth century's "metaphysical poets," those whose works evoked a quality of transcendence and deep religious feeling. His greatest work, *Centuries of Meditation*, was published only in the early twentieth century, and additional manuscripts of his poetry have also been rediscovered. This enlarged corpus of his work has led to renewed appreciation for his devotional and mystical reflections on creation. Today, new generations of theologians, mystics, and scientists are enthusiastically coming to value his significance as a devotional writer.

Traherne repeatedly evokes his experience of the natural world as he first encountered it in childhood:

> All appeared New, and Strange at the first, inexpressibly rare, and Delightfull, and Beautifull. I was a little Stranger which at my entrance into the world was Saluted and Surrounded with innumerable Joys....I saw all in the Peace of Eden; Heaven and Earth did sing my Creators Praises, and could not make more Melody to Adam, than to me. All Time was Eternity, and a Perpetual Sabbath. Is it not Strange, that an Infant should be Heir of the World, and see those Mysteries which the Books of the Learned never unfold?

Traherne bemoans the loss of favorable perceptions of nature in adulthood. This is caused, he argues, by a "bad education" that leads us to value a "globe of gold" far more than the "globe of earth." The loss here is more than childhood naiveté: it is a theological error as well.

> What ails Mankind to be so cross?
> The Useful Earth they count vile Dirt and Dross:
> 　　And neither prize
> 　　Its Qualities,
> Nor Donor's Lov. I fain would know
> How or why Men God's Goodness disallow.

On more than one occasion, arguing against his contemporaries who held that goodness is to be found only in heaven, Traherne made it clear that dismissing the divine goodness of creation is bad theology. When we do not cherish the world, we are not only going against our own nature as creatures who were made to love, we are denying the "excellencies" of God's love as it is manifested throughout creation. Traherne shares the tendency in Anglican thought to underscore the potential goodness of humanity. In *Centuries of Meditation* he directly challenges those who teach that humanity and creation itself are fallen. Instead, he insists that our sin lies not in loving the world "too much," but in loving humanity and the rest of creation "too little." God's love is the connective force that unites us to the world and to one another.[25]

Traherne recommends changing our perceptions of the world and of humanity through meditation. He does not do this glibly; he describes meditation as sweet but not easy. "Nothing," he writes, "is more Easy then to Think, so nothing is more Difficult then to Think Well." Still, he encourages us to persist by turning our sights on nature until we have "eyes to see" with cosmic consciousness:

> Till your Spirit filleth the whole World, and the Stars are your Jewels, till you are as Familiar with the Ways of God in all Ages as with your Walk and Table: till you are intimately Acquainted with that Shady Nothing out of which the World was made: till you lov Men so as to Desire their Happiness, with a Thirst equal to the zeal of your own: till you Delight in God for being Good to all: you never Enjoy the World.

Traherne expresses a sense of social felicity that is loving others more than oneself and prizing earth more than one's own home. For Traherne as well as for other Christian mystics, meditation is neither individualistic nor isolated from humanity. Rather, its intention is to evoke a desire for the happiness of others that surpasses personal concerns. This is the foundation for Traherne's ethical teaching on felicity.[26]

The child's delight in "all the excellency of things" persists throughout Traherne's work. So too does his insistence that the world is to be responsibly enjoyed and not despised as fallen. We should not be surprised to discover that Traherne's work is finding new followers among scientists today. For example, his description of "that Shady Nothing out of which the World was made" suggests the finding from quantum physics of the universe's origin in an unstable vacuum—that is, from "nothing." Traherne's sense of the infinitude and the "endlessly unsearchable" dimensions of the world fits with assumptions in contemporary astrophysics. Today's contemporary admirers echo a refrain that was apparent to Traherne's original audience: theology and science alike benefit from appreciating God's power in creation. As with Andrewes and Herbert, Traherne's focus on creation leads to a spiritual rediscovery of God's love and power.[27]

Andrewes, Herbert, and Traherne present us with rich resources for a creation-centered and sacramentally-grounded spirituality. These three Caroline divines spoke with the authority of tradition within the new and troubled culture of their day. Living amid the chaos of a "world turned upside down," they spoke of the divine unity and sacramental goodness of the universe. In their writings they left future generations of Anglicans a distinct theological legacy that embraces God's created order as a spiritual and material whole.

~ Reconsidering the Lilies

Late in her life Emily Dickinson, whose poems are steeped in the biblical and natural world, wrote: "Consider the lilies is the only commandment I ever obeyed." I applaud her bluntness. This, after all, is the same American poet who challenged the divines of her own day, "Why—do they shut me out of Heaven? Did I sing too loud?" The poet's capacity for looking and hearing are like those of the naturalist, the biologist, and the mystic. Dickinson's God, like the God known to the Caroline divines, saw creation intimately. Similarly, whether we are considering the lilies or studying fish, singing God's praises "in ev'ry corner" or trying to heed the warnings of today's ecologists, our perceptions about the world in which we live are by no means immaterial to our spiritual health.

The Caroline divines shaped a distinct tradition in Anglican spirituality. This sympathy with creation, however, seemed to disappear from general theological consciousness in the eighteenth century. The Enlightenment philosophy of science tended to view nature *not* as Hooker's source of divine wisdom, nor as Herbert's ingenious coupling of preservation with creation. The cosmos was not, as in Traherne, a delightfully mysterious teacher, but the servant of humanity. The natural world became an instrument to be quantified, taken apart, and put to use by man's rational mind. Tradition was distrusted in matters of rational inquiry. Gone was the sense of nature as a coherent organism of which we ourselves are a part. Some adherents of Enlightenment thought were "deists," believers who largely abandoned notions of God's further interest or intervention in the world. One modern historian of science aptly speaks of this historical period as reflecting "the death of nature."

Anglican teaching about the sacramental vision of the natural world did not come to the fore again until the end of the nineteenth century, with the publication of *Lux Mundi*. In the last chapter we saw how these essays helped Anglicans resolve critical differences over new methods of biblical study and new insights about the physical world. The *Lux Mundi* theologians consistently turned to the doctrine of the Incarnation to uphold the sanctification of all matter. In his essay on the sacraments, for example, Francis Paget points directly to the "sacramental principle" uniting the spiritual and material:

> And so through Sacramental elements and acts Christianity maintains its strong inclusive hold upon the whole of life. The consecration of material elements to be the vehicles of Divine grace keeps up on earth that vindication...which was achieved forever by the Incarnation and Ascension of Jesus Christ. We seem to see the material world rising from height to height; pierced, indeed, and, as it were, surprised at every stage by strange hints of a destiny beyond all likelihood.[28]

Paget's insistence on Christianity's "strong inclusive hold upon the whole of life" is reminiscent of the sacramental spirituality of the Caroline divines. With the *Lux Mundi* theologians we have come full circle, for they also succeeded in "recycling" theological perspectives in tune with the themes of grace and nature, God and humanity, that were so characteristic of sixteenth- and seventeenth-century Anglican thought.

I noted at the beginning of this chapter that the ecological crisis challenges fundamental theological assumptions about God, humanity, and the universe, but we also have valuable theological perspectives on creation within early Christian, medieval, and early modern Anglican thought. In "walking the bounds" of Anglican thought on creation, we have covered a lot of ground.

From this abundant harvest there are two fruitful lessons to be cherished most of all. The first pertains to our spiritual health. Some of our Anglican ancestors perceived

the universe as a material and spiritual whole. They refused to divide reality into separate spheres. Continuing
this tradition will be a challenge, given our tendencies to
oppose secular and spiritual concerns. Yet as Evelyn Underhill has reminded us, this is a matter of spiritual health as
well as theological integrity:

> Most of our conflicts and difficulties come from trying
> to deal with the spiritual and practical aspects of our life
> separately instead of realizing them as parts of one
> whole. If our practical life is centred on our own inter-
> ests, cluttered up by possessions, distracted by ambi-
> tions, passions, wants and worries,...we need not
> expect that our spiritual life will be a contrast to all this.
> The soul's house is not built on such a convenient plan:
> there are few soundproof partitions in it.

"The soul's house... [has] few soundproof partitions." I appreciate the direct simplicity of this metaphor. "See!" Underhill continues, "I am in all thing[s]! In the terrific
energies of the stellar universe, and in the smallest song of
the birds. In the seething struggle of modern industrial-
ism."[29] The presence of God's abiding reality can be difficult to recall amid the "loud pounding hammers" of the
world. Those of us who are comforted by seeing the "spiritual
and practical aspects" of our life as a whole can take heart
from this traditional emphasis within Anglican thought.

The second lesson to be cherished is the sacramental
grounding of Anglican spirituality. When we understand
God's presence in creation as one of *continuing* creativity
and redemption, we find that our faith is regularly enlivened through participation in the sacramental life. God's
greatness, grace, and calling are sacramentally celebrated
in the waters of baptism and the bread and wine of the
eucharist. God, humanity, and nature cooperate sacramen-

tally. God's incarnate presence is not restricted to humanity, but is carried and expressed in all things.

What does this sacramental legacy mean for us today? Toward the conclusion of the service of Holy Eucharist (Rite Two) the people say, "Send us out to do the work you have given us to do, to love and serve you as faithful witnesses of Christ our Lord" (BCP 366). This work will vary for each of us. Historian John Booty argues that by virtue of our incarnational emphasis and reliance on the sacraments, Anglicans are preeminently "ecologists." He writes: "Taking the Incarnation seriously involves Episcopalians in...taking creation seriously, entering into the human scene, and...striving to defend that creation against abuse." Simply stated, Christians who are nourished in the church's sacraments are called to respect and guard the dignity of creation.[30]

We have yet to discover how we can recycle these Anglican traditions in a practical way. Still, as we come to appreciate more fully the sacred character of creation—as we reconsider the lilies—we will be better prepared, and perhaps inspired as well, to bring the resources of our faith to the ecological decisions that lie before us.

Chapter Six

New Occasions Teach New Duties

S omeone once asked me if historians ever tired of looking at "old stuff." I replied that many of the materials I
worked with look "brand new" to me and to many of my
colleagues. My answer, I think, startled him. He had
thought that dusty manuscripts, ancient texts, old-time
concerns, and personalities from long ago were the primary job lot for historians. Of course, in some respects he is
correct. Ancient materials and subjects *are* familiar components of my profession, but so is a sense of newness and
discovery. Images of historical times can change as quickly
as our impressions of the present when new documents are
found, or young scholars with intriguing points of view
share their perceptions of a period. Even well-established
scholars change their minds from time to time. Eventually
new historical accounts appear and revised biographies are
written on persons we thought we knew well. Fresh interpretations and subjects are the lifeblood of those of us who
enjoy history. This is true whether we are scholars or ama-
teurs—that is, "lovers" of the past. Reading about the his-

tory of the church can deepen the inherent value and meaning of religious tradition, when we are touched by the freshness and wonder of our ancestors' conversations about God. Historians do not claim to know the full picture, and so we continue to look at materials old and new for fresh and abiding understanding.

In this book I have not provided a chronology of church history. Rather, I have selected a number of themes that I find important in understanding the Christian faith today, including the connection between tradition and change, how we envision the ministries of all the baptized, ways of dealing with conflict and disagreement, and theological resources that can be "recycled" to inform the pressing concerns of our own day. Much historical ground has been covered here; much more has not.

It is appropriate in a book entitled *Living with History* to reflect on tradition as a living thing and to pose various questions we might have about *our* place in history. Do we think of our lives as a part of the church's history? How can our historical and theological understandings assist us with everyday life in this world? Two short biographies will help our inquiry in this chapter, the stories of two exemplary Anglicans in the first half of the twentieth century, who put their faith to work amid the complexities and practical challenges they faced. What can we learn from their witness as we face a new millennium? Finally, I would like to close with a few practical suggestions for what to do when we disagree about tradition. These guidelines, informed by the history of Anglicanism, might prove useful in working through our inevitable disputes within the church community.

⌇ Living Tradition

In American life the Constitution of the United States is surely one of the most valuable, cherished, and often quoted sources of tradition. As the daughter of a lawyer who liked to discuss how Supreme Court justices made decisions, I enjoy reading about how the Court shifts in its handling of the Constitution over time. David Souter, a relatively new Supreme Court justice who is a New Englander and an Episcopalian, has caught my interest. Souter can be described as a justice who views the Constitution as a document that "evolves over time." Souter has cited in his decisions a legal axiom of Justice John Marshall Harlan (who served on the Court from 1955 to 1971): "Tradition is a living thing." Souter likewise values tradition for its living, flexible character. A pragmatist, he notes that the Court does not have to "decide [matters] for all time."[1] Even justices change their minds, making a decision at one time that may not prevail in another era. This reminds me of the stance taken in the Thirty-Nine Articles of Religion, specifically in the article "Of the Traditions of the Church," which speaks of the likelihood that traditions in the church will change "according to the diversity of countries, times, and men's manners" (BCP 874).

The founders of the Episcopal Church in the United States understood this principle well. Their handling of tradition has much to do with the current character of the Episcopal Church that we know today. Early American Episcopalians reshaped the royally-established church they had inherited from the Church of England. In their hands, tradition was alive and flexible; they both renewed it and set it aside. In the Constitution of the Protestant Episcopal Church in the United States of America (1792), they chose not to adopt the monarchical, established character of the church in England, but to create an American religious body that could exist alongside other denominations as an independent voluntary association. Within this American church, traditions of Anglican government, ministry, and liturgy were renewed in a body that, like the new Republic itself, was newly free of rule by the British empire. This does not mean that American Episcopalians were ambivalent about tradition. Rather, they discarded and rearranged tradition with a pragmatic flexibility that is reminiscent of Thomas Cranmer and (today) of David Souter. In their orientation toward the future, our Episcopal ancestors resembled other American churches in their "revolt against European church traditions." Significant new occasions at the end of the eighteenth century in this country led American Episcopalians to affirm new duties.[2]

"New occasions teach new duties." This phrase may sound familiar: it is from a hymn that has the muscular and memorable first line, "Once to every man and nation comes the moment to decide." One full verse of this hymn, from which I have taken the title and several subtitles for this chapter, is:

> By the light of burning martyrs
> Jesus' bleeding feet I track,
> Toiling up new Calvaries ever
> With the cross that turns not back
> New occasions teach new duties,
> Time makes ancient good uncouth;
> They must upward still and onward
> Who would keep abreast of truth.

"New occasions teach new duties, Time makes ancient good uncouth." This might seem an odd verse for a historian to admire. Yet as we explore the historical context for this verse, I think it will become clear why I find that it sets just the right tone for thinking about living with history well into the future.

The text of this hymn, which is no longer in the Episcopal hymnal, is from a poem called "The Present Crisis," written in 1845 by an American, James Russell Lowell. Lowell's poem concerns the freedom of nations and of slaves. His original poem begins:

> When a deed is done for freedom,
> through the broad earth's aching breast,
> Runs a thrill of joy prophetic,
> trembling on from east to west.[3]

For Lowell the "present crisis" was an unjust war with Mexico that he feared would extend slaveholding territory. We have already noted how some nineteenth-century Episcopalians used the Bible to defend slavery as an "ancient good." Lowell was adamant in 1845 that it was past time to move upward and beyond the evils of chattel slavery. The theological context of his poem, set at the foot of Calvary and devoted to humanity's freedom, honors the flexible character of tradition when it stands in the service of freedom: "They must upward still and onward Who would keep abreast of truth." Tradition, in the experience of many sincere and devout Episcopalians, is kept alive by moving upward and onward when significant new occasions, crises, and challenges call for new duties.

Decisions such as shaping the polity and worship of the church in a new land, whether or not to go to war, or how to end the practice of slavery in the new Republic represent major moments for shaping history. Yet history is not only concerned with highlighting what the old newsreels called "the big picture." Nor is history made only in times of profound change; history continues to be made in small, private moments as well. Most of us probably do not think of ourselves as a part of history. Yet we are all children of history. In an intriguing new book, *The Thread of Years*, John A. Lukacs reminds us that humanity is *not* divided into two different groups: one made up of regular people and the other of historical people. Lukacs writes, "Every event is a historical event; every source is a historical source; every person, a historical person."[4] Today there is a new democratic emphasis in historical consciousness. Similarly, when it comes to speaking about the cloud of witnesses who have shaped and continue to shape church history, we are all "historical persons." The histories of local parishes, for example, are actually shaped by the devotion, commitment, and activity of many persons, laity as well as clergy, as parish histories are starting to reflect.

There is yet another reason why you and I are a part of history. Those of us who call ourselves Christians become faithful "rememberers" in our baptism. In the words of the Baptismal Covenant, we pledge to "continue in the apostles' teaching." We remember the tradition not for the sake of the past alone nor to indulge in trivial nostalgia about the "good old days." Rather, memory within the body of Christ has to do with cost, with understanding, and with the future. The cost involves naming those, great and small, who have gone before us, and honoring their struggles, losses, and achievements. Knowledge of the church's past allows us to deepen our understanding of present times. The biblical record is replete with stories and historical lessons that our ancestors preserved as guidance for the future. Rowan Williams reminds us that remembrance "is the central image in the central act of Christian worship." In the Holy Eucharist we name "Jesus as the lord and judge on whom all lines of history converge."[5] Episcopalians profess this fullness of time as we pray:

We remember his death,
We proclaim his resurrection,
We await his coming in glory. (BCP 368)

Christians honor the past by living in the present and long-
ing for the promised future. Remembering is one of the important ways we live with one another and with God: as
Christians we are called to the sacred, sacramental task of
remembering.

⟿ Upward Still and Onward

As we begin to think of ourselves as a part of history, most
of us are more comfortable envisioning of ourselves as one
of the crowd, supporting others who are more directly engaged. Yet Martin Marty, a historian of American religion,
asserts, "We study history in order to intervene in history."[6] I think what Marty means here is that looking at
the past is a necessary part of preparing to act responsibly
as Christians in the future. Are we willing to think of ourselves as people who *intervene* in history, who are shaping
God's reign on earth? Within Anglicanism the tradition of
public responsibility, specifically of taking an active place
amid the cloud of witnesses who shape church and society,
is a significant theme. The established character of the
sixteenth-century Church of England supported the intention to build a "Godly Commonwealth" in England, and
four centuries later Evelyn Underhill's recommendation
that spirituality is "education for action" continued this
theme. Underhill, of course, would insist on balancing the
contemplative and active elements in our lives, but she saw
clearly the public character of a holy life. The findings of
Anglican theology and church history will not nourish
couch-potatoes—quite the reverse. The Baptismal Cove-

nant reminds us that we are expected to "strive for justice and peace among all people" (BCP 305).

Two Anglicans who lived out this call for public responsibility in the late nineteenth and early twentieth centuries were William Temple and Frances Perkins. Each entered the new century with a passionate commitment to tackle the industrial and economic evils of extreme poverty and harsh, unsafe labor conditions. Temple was an Anglican cleric and statesman who concluded his distinguished leadership of the Church of England as Archbishop of Canterbury. Perkins was an American stateswoman who, most notably as Secretary of Labor and the first woman Cabinet member, effectively and diligently shaped standards for labor and wage regulations. Each worked in the world to bring about the reign of God by contributing to a just society; each embodied the witness of the church at work in the world.

William Temple

William Temple was the second son of a bishop in the Church of England, Frederick Temple, who later became Archbishop of Canterbury. Throughout his life Temple's experience of society embraced people living in a variety of economic conditions. After teaching philosophy at Oxford he served as a schoolmaster at a private school, where he worked (not always successfully) to expand the number of working-class pupils. Temple then served as rector of a fashionable London parish and as a canon at Westminster Abbey, and was made bishop of the largely industrial diocese of Manchester in 1921. He was appointed to oversee England's Northern Province as Archbishop of York in 1929, where he served during a time of widespread economic depression, and was appointed as Archbishop of Canterbury in 1942. Admired as an influential theologian,

Temple made major contributions to the early twentieth-century ecumenical movement, worked on behalf of labor through the Workers' Educational Association, and wrote over twenty-five books on theological and social problems.

For Temple, as for earlier Anglican theologians like F. D. Maurice and William Augustus Muhlenberg, the suffering of chronically impoverished populations was a sign of theological breakdown. For these religious leaders care for the material needs of human society, along with sacramental worship and spiritual nurture, were essential components of the church's destiny and service. This theme was reflected in one of Temple's most popular books, *Christianity and Social Order*, first published in 1942 in the midst of the Second World War. Here Temple asserts that the church has not only a right but a duty to interfere in social issues, citing the doctrine of the Incarnation as his theological mandate. Temple knew that many did not agree with him, as he noted in the first sentence of the book: "The claim of the Christian Church to make its voice heard in matters of politics and economics is very widely resented, even by those who are Christian in personal belief and devotional practice."[7] Still, he insisted that our biblical and historical calling involves inculcating Christian principles within the economic order, as well as advocating systemic change in the name of justice. Christianity, he exclaimed in another essay, "is the most avowedly materialist of all the great religions."[8] Temple's theological vision, as another twentieth-century Archbishop of Canterbury, Michael Ramsey, has observed, included all of experience: "Everything was related to God." Accordingly, Temple cautioned against spending "the whole of our activity" in worship. He urged spending the "greater part of our time," the other six days of the week, expressing God's love through service in the world.[9]

Frances Perkins

Frances Perkins embodied William Temple's advocacy of a conscientious involvement in the affairs of the world. This remarkable American leader and social reformer held a life-long interest in improving conditions among American workers. Raised in New England and a graduate of Mount Holyoke College, Perkins was influenced in the first decade of the twentieth century by the practices of social service and public policy pursued in Chicago's settlement houses, especially Hull House. She went on to work for urban social reform in Philadelphia and New York City, studying economics and sociology at Columbia and writing an article on undernourished children in 1910. Her career in social reform and labor relations evolved into political service in the government of New York State, where she worked effectively for passage of a bill to restrict working hours for women to fifty-four, and later forty-eight hours a week. From 1933 to 1945 she served in President Roosevelt's Cabinet as Secretary of Labor. Her term in this national office coincided with the greatest period of labor unrest and economic dislocation in America. Although controversial, Perkins proved to be adroit in proposing and implementing New Deal legislation. Her legislative strategies included Social Security insurance, wage-and-hour regulations, unemployment insurance, and measures for abolishing child labor. She concluded her career at the age of eighty-three as a popular university lecturer and college professor working in the area of industrial and labor relations.

Perkins's vocation for social reform was deeply and clearly informed by her faith; she bluntly stated that her commitment to industrial reform was prompted by more than a mere humanitarian urge, and as a young settlement worker in Chicago she argued that social reform was explicitly "for Jesus' sake." Raised by devoted Congregationalists, Perkins became a devout Anglo-Catholic during her early years in Chicago. As Secretary of Labor she made regular retreats with a small community of Episcopal nuns in Maryland, spending most of her time in prayer and silence but occasionally discussing complex matters of social legislation with the convent's superior. After her retirement from the Cabinet, Perkins spoke more openly of her faith and of the church's obligation to "build a good society and prepare the Kingdom of Heaven on earth." This theme is also emphasized in her 1948 parish lectures on "The Christian in the World."

As with Temple, the Incarnation provided Perkins with "the great and mighty principle" that grounded the purpose of Christian society. Our destiny, she claims, is "to know, love and serve God." Again, like Temple, Perkins insisted that the church's role is to inform the consciences of the people and to underscore the moral implications of their choices. Her steadfast faith and active moral conscience supported and propelled her search for justice for all workers. Her obituary in the *New York Times* included her direct and telling confession of her sustenance: "I don't see how people who don't believe in God can go on in this world as it is today." Perkins was an inspirational lay leader, a dedicated public official, and a devout and conscientious believer. Throughout her life, she moved upward and onward, seeking to shape effective ethical stands on matters of social consequence.[10]

Temple and Perkins embody the responsibility of furthering God's reign on earth. They were public figures, well-known leaders whose faithfulness as Christians guided them to active lives of service. While few of us will achieve their greatness, their witness can inspire us all. Should we show our faith in public? Temple and Perkins certainly did. Drawing upon their formative identity as

Anglican Christians, they affirmed the church's involvement in the affairs of the world. We will not all be public leaders, yet involvement in the affairs of the world is far from optional for Anglicans. How will we choose to intervene in a new century? Will we draw upon our past, learning from our mistakes and recalling the effective witness of those who have gone before? Will we "study history in order to intervene in history?" As we stand at the end of this century and look forward to a new millennium, Temple and Perkins represent two of many saints whose witness and service are well worth embracing as our own.

～ Keeping Abreast of Truth

Keeping "abreast of truth," as Lowell's poem puts it, is a challenging responsibility. For many of us who live at the end of this century, keeping up with the seemingly relentless pace of change is hard enough. Many Anglicans who deeply cherish their religious traditions are afraid that change is overwhelming those traditions. It may help us to know that other ages have shared this sense of loss: in 500 B.C.E., for example, Heraclitus wrote, "Nothing endures but change." We are left with a conundrum. A devotion to tradition can become painful when traditions change.

When I first began to explore the topic of tradition, I wanted to learn more about the beliefs and attitudes of local parishioners toward tradition and change, knowing it would elicit strong feelings. So I invited adult learners from a nearby parish to explore this subject during the Lenten season. When I asked the group of about thirty-five Episcopalians what their continuing concerns were, one member responded, "Traditions and customs are extremely meaningful, and when they change, they are hurtful and hard to accept. Who is responsible? Why are we expected to change and like it?" These are tough questions that lie at the heart of being a member of a Christian community. In response to this plea I wish to highlight several important elements—seven guidelines consonant with Anglican tradition—that can be used in the process of discussing controversial matters.

1. Seek common ground.
What can we positively agree upon that is central to our identity? When we are involved in controversies over tradition and customs, this is one excellent strategy. Being clear about our most valued beliefs and traditions allows us to move forward as a people of faith. Our early American ancestors found common ground for shaping the new Episcopal Church according to those practices and beliefs upon which they could agree. This is a helpful component for mediating all sorts of conversations about religious difference, including ecumenical dialogues.

A shared orientation to what is of ultimate importance in our lives of faith can be hard work these days because the Episcopal Church, like other churches, has a history of unjust, oppressive, and exclusive traditions. When serious conflicts and debates over a particular issue escalate, it is a good idea to put shared covenants on the table. Looking for common ground can be a helpful way to move forward. This allows us to make room for wider understanding and encourages more constructive conversations.

2. Value conversation.
This may sound obvious, but it is not easy. In today's society there are few concrete places where people of radically different views meet face to face to talk across the political and social spectrum. We may well be out of practice in respectfully talking and listening in the midst of serious divisions. Yet members of the same denomination are expected

to stick together even when we talk about substantive and potentially explosive issues at parish and diocesan meetings and church conventions. How can we learn to have conversations that are both honest and conciliatory? Such dialogue includes the recognition of contradictory views held by members of the same church. William Temple and other Anglicans have traditionally drawn pragmatic connections between plain speaking and productive doing. As Temple observes in *Christianity and Social Order,* "By talking we gradually form public opinion, and public opinion, if it is strong enough, gets things done."[11]

3. Seek the broadest understanding.

Comprehensiveness is a traditional and favored concept in Anglican history. For example, it was a central strategy of seventeenth-century Restoration leaders of the church and state as they labored to shape documents that would unite the nation and encompass a wide variety of religious beliefs. Our history repeatedly teaches us that truth is larger than any one perspective, and the 1968 Lambeth Conference embraced this central Anglican guideline: "Comprehensiveness implies a willingness to allow liberty of interpretation, with a certain slowness in arresting or restraining exploratory thinking."[12]

William Temple once discouraged drawing "sharply defined boundaries" in the church. This is a similar intent to Anglican theologian Rowan Greer's description of Anglicanism:

> More persuasive to me is the idea of Anglicanism as a conversation—or even an argument—with different voices speaking for scripture, for tradition, for reason, and for experience. Or, to put it another way, it seems to me that conflict in the church need not be an evil and

that the church needs both those who wish to preserve its heritage and those who are concerned that it move forward. The foot-draggers and the banner-wavers may well both be necessary.[13]

I like envisioning Anglicanism as "a conversation" with "different voices speaking for scripture, for tradition, for reason, and for experience." This rings true to my assessment of the sixteenth-century church of the English Reformation, as well as the Episcopal Church today. It is helpful to envision Anglicanism as a dialogue that searches faithfully for comprehensive understanding.

4. Appreciate ambiguity.
A sincere appreciation for ambiguity has long been a significant component in the historical and theological life of the Anglican church, and is an important and humbling asset in church conversations. Theologically, when it comes to stating what we know of God, ambiguity is essential. Historically, both Thomas Cranmer and Queen Elizabeth I promoted theological assertions about the Lord's Supper that allowed a variety of interpretations, including ambiguous ones, to be affirmed. In the church today, Verna Dozier believes that a traditionally Anglican recognition of ambiguity is endangered by those who currently believe they have "the final answer." In a recent interview she noted: "What the world needs are people who are humble enough to know they are not God and don't have absolute answers and are acceptable even though they don't." Bishop Frederick Borsch believes that "in the midst of the messiness, the incongruities and surprises and ongoing dialogue and exploration, there can be some of the greatest opportunities for the Holy Spirit to enter into our lives."[14] Comprehensiveness and ambiguity are essential theologi-

cal companions for expressing the wonder and mystery of God's presence in our lives.

5. *Make room for imagination.*

It is not appropriate for Anglicans, as we have noted, to "make up" history to suit the present mode—this dishonors the past. Yet part of thinking through a difficult issue is imagining other possibilities for the future. Our American ancestors at the end of the eighteenth century tested and sifted various information and possibilities until they had created a new church in a new land. It is no wonder that the arts, especially music and poetry, have an important place in shaping Anglican spirituality. Through their writings, poets and spiritual leaders, including Julian of Norwich, George Herbert, John Donne, and Evelyn Underhill, have attempted to express the inexpressible. Herbert praises church music for showing us "the way to heaven's door."[15] As we have seen, making music together—offering hymns of prayer and praise—excites our sense of wonder, love, and praise.

6. *Ask questions.*

This present age is exhausted by data. Sometimes I feel like Gilbert and Sullivan's Modern Major General: I am not sure what to do with all the "information: vegetable, animal, and mineral" that this society seems to collect. As any good researcher knows, data by itself does not provide answers. We have noticed how the study of history invites us to keep asking questions. When we begin studying the Bible, sometimes one question leads to another, and to yet another. This is an ancient and honorable way of teaching: in the gospels Jesus frequently responds to a challenge or question not with an answer, but with questions. Thoughtful inquiries need to be welcomed continually among people of faith. In the Anglican tradition this even includes asking questions about well-established beliefs and customs. No one wants to get stuck in time, letting today alone define what is possible. A wise lay leader in Vermont once observed that our society today suffers from theological heart disease: not hardening of the arteries but hardening of the categories. Asking questions is one way Christians explore new occasions and inquire into new duties.

7. Encourage one another.

Christians are not famous for treating one another with kindness. Despite repeated biblical injunctions to love and to forgive, observers from the earliest centuries of Christian life to the present times have taunted us for the way we treat one another. "See how they love one another!" is typically *not* a compliment in religious communities. Perhaps this is why the letter to the Hebrews, among other epistles, insists that we are most pleasing to God when we "let mutual love continue" (13:1).

Similarly, Anglican theologians have also offered words of encouragement to the church. Thomas Cranmer advocated treating even those with whom we strongly disagree in a friendly and charitable fashion. Richard Hooker spoke of a God who works first of all by love and mercy, and not by fear. F. D. Maurice taught in the midst of the nineteenth-century industrial revolution that cooperation, not competition, is our intended destiny. Offering words of encouragement to one another in these latter days is a fine way to honor this tradition.

Here is a concluding exercise. Let me see if these seven touchstones can help me respond to a difficult question about Episcopal Church history: Is the Episcopal Church a traditional church? As you might suspect, a legitimate response is: "Yes, and no!" By "yes," I mean that as a living and faithful body, the church is deeply formed and sustained by tradition. Tradition functions with authority as an ongoing and future part of our identity. By "no," I mean that there is no *one* "traditional" understanding of the Episcopal Church, or of Anglicanism in general. We cannot—historically or currently—describe a *fixed* content for Anglicanism. This response raises additional questions. Can we imagine ways of carrying our respect for tradition into the future? In any event, the conversation about tradition and change will continue, as we encourage one another to deepen our understandings of living with history.

Endnotes

∿ Chapter 1: Living with History

1. See Paul Avis, "What is 'Anglicanism'?" in *The Study of Anglicanism*, Stephen Sykes, John Booty, and Jonathan Knight, eds., rev. ed. (Minneapolis: Fortress, 1998), 459-476.

2. Geoffrey W. Bromiley, "Tradition and Traditions in Thomas Cranmer," *Anglican and Episcopal History* 59 (1990), 475. I have also drawn upon another fine article in the same volume of this journal by John E. Booty, "Tradition and Traditions," 453-466.

3. Richard Holloway, "'Behold: I Make All Things New,'" in *Living Tradition: Affirming Catholicism in the Anglican Church*, ed. Jeffrey John (Cambridge, Mass.: Cowley, 1992), 127.

4. See Hooker's arguments about change in the church's life in *Of the Laws of Ecclesiastical Polity*, Georges Edelen, ed. *The Folger Library Edition of the Works of Richard Hooker*, W. Speed Hill, ed., vol. 2 (Cambridge, Mass.: Belknap Press, 1977), V.8-9.

∿ Chapter 2: Ten Touchstones of History

1. For a fuller exploration of the Incarnation in our lives, see my *Courageous Incarnation* (Cambridge, Mass.: Cowley, 1993).

2. On the centrality of the Incarnation in Ramsey's theology see Kenneth Leech, "'The Real Archbishop': A Profile of Michael Ramsey," *Christian Century* (March 12, 1986), 266-269.

3. Hooker, *Laws*, V.54.5.

4. Elizabeth O'Conner, *Cry Pain, Cry Hope* (Washington, D. C.: The Servant Leadership School, 1987), 169.

5. Charles Gore, "The Holy Spirit and Inspiration," in *Lux Mundi: A Series of Studies in the Religion of the Incarnation*, Charles Gore, ed. (New York: John W. Lowell, 1889), 269.

6. *John Donne: Selections from Divine Poems, Sermons, Devotions, and Prayers*, John Booty, ed. (New York: Paulist Press, 1990), 271.

7. Stephen Sykes, *Unashamed Anglicanism* (Nashville: Abingdon Press, 1995), 14, 189.

8. Cited in John Francis Potter and William J. Wolf, eds., *Toward the Recovery of Unity: The Thought of Frederick Denison Maurice* (New York: Seabury Press, 1964), 83.

9. David Daniell, *William Tyndale: A Biography* (New Haven: Yale University Press, 1994), 1.

10. Cited in Diarmaid MacCulloch, *Thomas Cranmer: A Life* (New Haven: Yale University Press, 1996), 461.

11. Stephen Neill, *Anglicanism* (New York: Oxford University Press, 1978), 285.

12. Mary Sudman Donovan, *A Different Call: Women's Ministries in the Episcopal Church, 1850-1920* (Wilton, Conn.: Morehouse-Barlow, 1986), 11. See also Pamela W. Darling, *New Wine: The Story of Women Transforming Leadership and Power in the Episcopal Church* (Cambridge, Mass.: Cowley, 1994).

13. Quoted in David E. Sumner, *The Episcopal Church's History: 1945-1985* (Wilton, Conn.: Morehouse-Barlow, 1987), 10.

14. *Jeremy Taylor*, Thomas K. Carroll, ed. (New York: Paulist Press, 1990), 440, 445.

15. This quotation has been attributed to Toni Morrison.

ᔐ Chapter 3: The Ministry We Share

1. Verna J. Dozier, *The Dream of God: A Call to Return* (Cambridge, Mass.: Cowley, 1991), 142, 140.

2. Michael G. Lawler and Thomas J. Shanahan, *Church: A Spirited Communion* (Collegeville, Minn.: Liturgical Press, 1995), 73. My

assessments of early Christian and medieval understandings of ministry, church, and laity are largely informed by their scholarship.

3. Dozier, *Dream of God*, 148.

4. Quoted in Marianne Arbogast, "Liberating the Baptized: Shared Ministry in Northern Michigan," *The Witness* (August/September, 1994), 11.

5. Rowan Williams, *A Ray of Darkness* (Cambridge, Mass.: Cowley, 1994), 149.

6. Kathleen Norris, *Dakota: A Spiritual Geography* (Boston: Houghton Mifflin, 1993), 105.

7. Evelyn Underhill, *The Life of the Spirit and the Life of Today* (Harrisburg, Penn.: Morehouse, 1994), xi, 118.

8. Ibid., 118, 150, 224, 219.

9. Ibid., 32-33, 37-38.

10. *A Keeper of the Word: Selected Writings*, Bill Wylie Kellermann, ed. (Grand Rapids: William B. Eerdmans, 1994). Other essays on Stringfellow are found in *Radical Christian and Exemplary Lawyer: Honoring William Stringfellow*, Andrew W. McThenia, Jr., ed. (Grand Rapids: William B. Eerdmans, 1995); and *Prophet of Justice, Prophet of Life: Essays on William Stringfellow*, Robert Boak Slocum, ed. (New York: Church Publishing, 1997).

11. Kellermann, *Keeper of the Word*, 20, 31, 71, 172.

12. Ibid., 117, 12, 163.

13. Ibid., 71, 182, 322-323.

14. Verna Dozier, *The Authority of the Laity* (Washington, D. C.: The Alban Institute, 1982), 3.

15. Dozier, *Dream of God*, 145.

16. Verna Dozier, *The Calling of the Laity: Verna Dozier's Anthology* (Washington, D. C.: The Alban Institute, 1988), 115-116; and see Kellermann, *Keeper of the Word*, 159.

17. Dozier, *The Calling of the Laity*, 111-112, 115.

18. Dozier, *Dream of God*, 139, 133, 150.

19. I am grateful for Dr. Willie's assistance in providing me with copies of his sermons and other unpublished materials. See also Charles V. Willie, "Getting a Handle on Institutional Sin," *The Witness* (March 1981), 17-18.

20. Charles V. Willie, *Race, Ethnicity, and Socioeconomic Status* (Bayside, N. Y.: General Hall, 1983), 9, 16.

21. Charles V. Willie, "The Priesthood of All Believers," unpublished sermon (July 29, 1974), 4, 6, 8.

22. Charles V. Willie, "Women Bishops? No Question About It," *The Witness* (March 1988), 17.

~ Chapter 4: Living with Controversy

1. Lacey Baldwin Smith, *Elizabeth Tudor: Portrait of a Queen* (Boston: Little, Brown, 1975), 106.

2. William P. Haugaard, *Elizabeth and the English Reformation: The Struggle for a Stable Settlement of Religion* (Cambridge: Cambridge University Press, 1968), 290; see also 333-338.

3. Ibid., 329-330. This is Francis Bacon's description of Queen Elizabeth's policies.

4. Cited in Paul Avis, *Anglicanism and the Christian Church* (Minneapolis: Fortress Press, 1989), 54.

5. Richard Hooker, *Tractates and Sermons*, ed. Laetitia Yeandle and Egil Grislis, *The Folger Library Edition of the Works of Richard Hooker*, W. Speed Hill, ed., vol. 5 (Cambridge, Mass.: Belknap Press, 1990), 169, 640-641. I have modernized the spelling in the concluding paragraph of this sermon on "Justification."

6. Quoted in Smith, *Elizabeth Tudor*, 106.

7. Robert Pinsky, *An Explanation of America* (Princeton: Princeton University Press, 1979), 8.

8. See the summary of Bishop Leighton Coleman's assessment by Chester Forester Dunham, *The Attitude of the Northern Clergy Toward the South, 1860-1865* (Philadelphia: Porcupine Press, 1974), 20-21.

9. Gardiner H. Shattuck, Jr., "Repeating the Past," *The Living Church* (June 16, 1991), 12. In my analysis I have largely chosen to follow Shattuck's interpretive expertise on religion during the Civil War, and I am grateful for his assistance and advice. Any errors in this account remain my own.

10. Cited by Shattuck, "Repeating the Past," 12.

11. In this brief summary I have drawn upon J. Carlton Hayden, "After the War: The Mission and Growth of the Episcopal Church Among Blacks in the South, 1865-1877," *The Historical Magazine of the Protestant Episcopal Church* (December 1973), 403-427; and David L. Holmes, *A Brief History of the Episcopal Church* (Valley Forge, Penn.: Trinity Press International, 1993), 78-87.

12. Cited in Dunham, *Attitude of the Northern Clergy*, 88; see also 99-100. I have used Dunham extensively for quotations from Episcopalians on slavery and abolition.

13. Ibid., 106-108, 101.

14. Quotations from the two Pastoral Letters of 1862 (and convenient access to other documents from the Civil War) may be found in Don S. Armentrout and Robert Boak Slocum, eds., *Documents of Witness: A History of the Episcopal Church, 1782-1985* (New York: Church Hymnal, 1994), 161, 163, 158-173 *passim*.

15. Ibid., 165, 169-170.

16. Ibid., 179-180. This sermon was preached by Morgan Dix on October 29, 1865.

17. Dunham, *Attitude of the Northern Clergy*, 20-21, 100-101, 149; and Gardiner H. Shattuck, Jr., *A Shield and Hiding Place: The Religious Life of the Civil War Armies* (Macon, Ga.: Mercer University Press, 1987), 9, 135.

18. See Hayden, "After the War," 413, 410-419.

19. See Holmes, *A Brief History*, 71-74; and Owanah Anderson, *400 Years: Anglican/Episcopal Mission Among American Indians* (Cincinnati: Forward Movement, 1997).

20. Shattuck, *Shield and Hiding Place*, 3, 135.

21. "Letter from the Birmingham City Jail," cited in *A Testament of Hope: The Essential Writings of Martin Luther King, Jr.*, James Melvin Washington, ed. (San Francisco: Harper & Row, 1986), 295; and W. E. B. Du Bois, *The Souls of Black Folk* (Chicago: A. C. McClurg, 1903), 13.

22. Robert M. Young, "The Impact of Darwin on Conventional Thought," in *The Victorian Crisis of Faith*, Anthony Synomdson, ed. (London: SPCK, 1970), 19, 27, 31.

23. *Lux Mundi*, ix. For an excellent assessment of *Lux Mundi* and its impact on Anglican theology see Arthur Michael Ramsey, *An Era in Anglican Theology* (New York: Charles Scribner's Sons, 1960), 1-15.

24. From *Lux Mundi*, 151, 80-84; and Charles Gore, *The Reconstruction of Belief: Belief in God, Belief in Christ, the Holy Spirit and the Church* (New York: Charles Scribner's Sons, 1926), 188. See also the introductory essay by Tess Cosslett, ed., in *Science and Religion in the Nineteenth Century* (Cambridge: Cambridge University Press, 1984), 15-20.

25. *Lux Mundi*, 285, 297, 302.

26. Frederick Houk Borsch, *Outrage and Hope: A Bishop's Reflections in Times of Change and Challenge* (Valley Forge, Penn.: Trinity Press International, 1996), 82-86.

27. John Polkinghorne, *Serious Talk: Science and Religion in Dialogue* (Valley Forge, Penn.: Trinity Press International, 1995), viii, 17, 62, 64; also see John Polkinghorne, *Belief in God in an Age of Science* (New Haven: Yale University Press, 1998).

～ Chapter 5: Recycling Tradition

1. See the *State of the World* (Washington, D. C.: Worldwatch Institute, 1990), 172-190.

2. David Jenkins, *God, Politics, and the Future* (Wilton, Conn.: Morehouse-Barlow, 1988), 74.

3. Kwok Pui Lan, "Ecology and the Recycling of Christianity," *The Ecumenical Review* 44 (1992), 304-307.

4. See, for example, the influential article by Lynn White, "The Historical Roots of Our Ecological Crisis," *Science* 155 (1967), 1203-1207.

5. Quoted by Kathleen Norris in *The Cloister Walk* (New York: Riverhead Books, 1996), 295.

6. A. M. Allchin, "The Theology of Nature in the Eastern Fathers and among Anglican Theologians," *Man and Nature*, Hugh Montefiore, ed. (London: Collins, 1976), 146, 143-154. This book contains the 1974 report and essays on the environment by a working group of the Doctrine Commission of the Church of England. It is one of the first texts to focus on the relevance of Anglican doctrine for thinking about ecology. I have largely followed its conclusions on Anglican theology.

7. Hymn 210 in *The Hymnal 1982* (New York: Church Hymnal, 1985). See also Hymns 198 and 199, with words attributed to John of Damascus.

8. There is debate about which of these ecological imperatives is most helpful. See, for example, René Dubose, "Franciscan Conservation versus Benedictine Stewardship" in David and Eileen Spring, eds., *Ecology and Religion in History* (New York: Harper & Row, 1974), 119-136. Francis' "Canticle of the Sun" is Hymn 406 in *The Hymnal 1982*.

9. *Julian of Norwich, Showings*, Edmund Colledge and James Walsh, eds. (New York: Paulist Press, 1978), 183, 293-299, 192.

10. Hooker, *Laws*, II.1.4.

11. Ibid., V.56.5.

12. Hooker, *Tractates and Sermons*, 333. I have modernized the spelling in this quotation, which is taken from his sermon on the "Nature of Pride."

13. My interpretation of Hooker's influence on Anglican thinking about creation is informed by A. M. Allchin, "The Theology of Nature," 149, 150-152.

14. Hymn 580 in *The Hymnal 1982*. "Earth and all stars" is Hymn 412; "All things bright and beautiful" is Hymn 405.

15. I am again indebted to the scholarship of A. M. Allchin; see his essay "Lancelot Andrewes," in *The English Religious Tradition and the Genius of Anglicanism*, Geoffrey Rowell, ed. (Oxford: IKON, 1992), 145-164.

16. The Andrewes' citations are from *The Private Devotions of Lancelot Andrewes*, trans. F. E. Brightman (New York: Meridian Books, 1961), 7. See also Stephen W. Sykes, "The Fundamentals of Christianity" in *The Study of Anglicanism*, 267.

17. See Allchin, "Lancelot Andrewes," 145-146; and *The Private Devotions*, 59, lviii.

18. Ibid., xlviii, 63.

19. On Herbert's contemporary reputation see Elizabeth Clarke, "George Herbert's *The Temple*: The Genius of Anglicanism and the Inspiration for Poetry," in Rowell, *English Religious Tradition*, 127-131.

20. *George Herbert: The Country Parson, The Temple*, John N. Wall, Jr., ed. (New York: Paulist Press, 1981), 242-243, 168, 107.

21. Ibid., 135, 165-166.

22. Ibid., 311.

23. Paul Elmen, "Anglican Morality" in *The Study of Anglicanism*, 366.

24. *George Herbert*, 168.

25. See the collected edition of his works, *Thomas Traherne: Poems, Centuries and Three Thanksgivings*, Anne Ridler, ed. (London: Oxford University Press, 1966), 263, 267, 113-114, 243-244. I have followed Ridler in Traherne's irregular spelling and punctuation.

26. Ibid., 169, 177-178.

27. See Don Rehkopf, "Thomas Traherne: A Visionary for the Laboratory," *Christian Century*, 103 (1986), 693-694; John Noffsinger, "Thomas Traherne and the Recovery of God," *Journal of Religious Studies* 18 (1992), 125-133; and Graham Dowell, *Enjoying the World: The Rediscovery of Thomas Traherne* (London: Mowbray, 1990).

28. *Lux Mundi*, 353.

29. Evelyn Underhill, *The Spiritual Life* (Wilton, Conn.: Morehouse-Barlow, 1955), 33; and *The Life of the Spirit and the Life of Today*, 16.

30. John Booty, *The Episcopal Church in Crisis* (Cambridge, Mass.: Cowley, 1988), 148.

~ Chapter 6: New Occasions Teach New Duties

1. See material about Souter and Harlan in John Aloysius Farrell, "Scales of Justice," *Boston Globe Magazine* (May 10, 1998), 17-18, 23-24.

2. William A. Clebsch, "American Churches as Traducers of Tradition," *Anglican Theological Review* 53 (1971), 27-31.

3. Lowell's poem, "The Present Crisis," is partially quoted in *The Hymnal 1940 Companion*, 2nd ed. rev. (New York: The Church Pension Fund, 1949), 312. It is Hymn 519 in *The Hymnal 1940*.

4. John A. Lukacs, *The Thread of Years* (New Haven: Yale University Press, 1998), 3.

5. Williams, *A Ray of Darkness*, 209, 206-207.

6. See Martin Marty's introduction to Booty's *Episcopal Church in Crisis*, 7.

7. William Temple, *Christianity and Social Order* (London: Shepheard-Walwyn, 1987), 29, 32.

8. William Temple, *Nature, Man and God* (London: Macmillan, 1964), 478.

9. See Arthur Michael Ramsey's assessment of Temple in *An Era in Anglican Theology* (New York: Charles Scribners' Sons, 1960), 146; and *William Temple, The Church and Its Teaching To-day* (New York: Macmillan, 1936), 17-18.

10. See George Martin, *Madam Secretary: Frances Perkins* (Boston: Houghton Mifflin, 1976), 57-58, 279-283; and Perkins' essay "Full Employment" in *Christianity Takes a Stand: An Approach to the Issues of Today*, William Scarlett, ed. (New York: Penguin, 1946), 108, 98, 94-109.

11. Temple, *Christianity*, 114.

12. *The Lambeth Conference, 1968: Resolutions and Reports* (SPCK and Seabury Press, 1968), 140.

13. Rowan Greer, "Anglicanism as an Ongoing Argument," *The Witness* (May, 1998), 23.

14. See Julie A. Wortman, "Ambiguity and Conflict: An Interview with Verna Dozier," *The Witness* (May, 1998), 22; and Borsch, *Outrage and Hope*, 151.

15. Herbert's poem "Church Music" may be found in *George Herbert*, 181-182.

Resources

~ **General Reference Works**

No matter how good a memory you have for names and dates, everyone needs a few good general reference books for the history of Christianity. Two reference works that Episcopalians often use are *The Oxford Dictionary of the Christian Church*, 3rd ed. (Oxford University Press, 1997) and *The Oxford Illustrated History of Christianity* (Oxford University Press, 1990). The latter volume contains chapters on Christianity and Islam, as well as Christianity in Latin America, Africa, and Asia, Great Britain, Europe, and North America.

Justo L. González's two-volume paperback history, *The History of Christianity* (Harper, 1985) is also a good choice. It includes the growth of Christianity outside the European mainstream and explores the social, political, and economic movements that formed its context. Another broad approach is furnished by *Christianity: A Social and Cultural History* (Macmillan, 1991), a one-volume history by Howard Clark Kee, Mark Noll, and others. Ronald Takaki's *A Different Mirror: A History of Multicultural America* (Little, Brown, 1993) is a brilliant and informative revisionist history of America.

～ English Reformation History

The best place to start on reading English Reformation history is A. G. Dickens' *The English Reformation*, 2nd ed. (Pennsylvania State University Press, 1989), which provides a detailed history of the period through 1559. A useful collection of essays on this period, edited by John E. Booty, is *The Godly Kingdom of Tudor England: Great Books of the English Reformation* (Morehouse-Barlow, 1981).

Several biographies of influential leaders of the era are also helpful. Among them, Susan Doran's *Elizabeth I and Religion, 1558-1603* (Routledge, 1994) is excellent. See also Diarmaid MacCulloch, *Thomas Cranmer, A Life* (Yale University Press, 1996) and Lacey Baldwin Smith, *Elizabeth Tudor: Portrait of a Queen* (Little, Brown, 1975).

～ Episcopal Church History

Two histories of the Episcopal Church have been published recently and both are well worth reading: Robert W. Prichard's *A History of the Episcopal Church* (Morehouse, 1991) and David Holmes' *A Brief History of the Episcopal Church* (Trinity Press International, 1993). Professor Holmes' history is particularly well-written and has excellent photographs. Don Armentrout and Robert Boak Slocum's *Documents of Witness* (Church Hymnal, 1994) brings together readings from primary sources in the history of the Episcopal Church from 1782 to 1985.

Other good scholarly studies of the history of the Episcopal Church are also available. John Woolverton's *Colonial Anglicanism in North America* (Wayne State University Press, 1984) is a thorough account of the colonial churches in America. Diana Hochstedt Butler's *Standing Against the Whirlwind* (Oxford University Press, 1995) studies the evangelical party in the Episcopal Church and its effect on the piety, identity, theology, and mission of the church, while Robert Bruce Mullin's *Episcopal Vision/American Reality* (Yale University Press, 1986) examines the high church vision as exemplified in the figure of John Henry Hobart, bishop of New York. A book by Allen C. Guelzo, *For the Union of Evangelical Christendom* (Pennsylvania State University Press, 1994), also explores evangelicalism through the history of the Reformed Episcopal Church. Robert W. Prichard's *The Nature of Salvation: Theological Consensus in the Episcopal Church, 1801-1873* (University of Illinois Press, 1997) studies high church and evangelical theology in the nineteenth-century Episcopal Church. All five books are excellent examples of the good and accessible historical scholarship available from university presses.

For the history of women in the Episcopal Church, Catherine Prelinger's *Episcopal Women: Gender, Spirituality, and Commitment in an American Mainline Denomination* (Oxford University Press, 1992) is an excellent resource, bringing together essays by women scholars in religious history and sociology. Mary Sudman Donovan's *A Different Call* (Morehouse, 1986) looks at lay women's ministries in the church between 1850 and 1920, while Pamela W. Darling's *New Wine* (Cowley, 1994) examines the history of the leadership and ordination of women in the Episcopal Church and the consecration of the first woman bishop.

Joanna Bowen Gillespie's *Women Speak: Of God, Congregations, and Change* (Trinity Press International, 1995) is a sociological study of the women's movement and the church, which I recommend particularly because of its work with women's history in congregations. Pauli Murray has written on her experiences as an African-American woman in *Pauli Murray: The Autobiography of a Black Activist, Feminist, Lawyer, Priest, and Poet* (University of Tennessee Press, 1989).

Recent important biographies of Episcopal church leaders include Will D. Campbell's *And Also With You: Duncan Gray and the American Dilemma* (Providence House, 1998); John F. Woolverton's *The Education of Phillips Brooks* (University of Illinois Press, 1998); and John Booty's *An American Apostle: The Life of Stephen Fielding Bayne, Jr.* (Trinity Press International, 1998).

The primary history of rural ministry in the Episcopal Church is found in *Vision Fulfilling: The Story of Rural and Small Community Work of the Episcopal Church During the Twentieth Century* (Morehouse, 1987) by William Davidson, Leo Maxwell Brown, and Allen Brown.

The most comprehensive work on the history of black Episcopalians is Harold T. Lewis' *Yet With A Steady Beat: The African American Struggle for Recognition in the Episcopal Church* (Trinity Press International, 1996). Edward W. Rodman's *Let There Be Peace Among Us: A Story of the Union of Black Episcopalians* (Union of Black Episcopalians, 1990) also handles this question. On Native Americans and the Episcopal church, see the recent and critically helpful study by Owanah Anderson, *400 Years: Anglican/Episcopal Mission Among American Indians* (Forward Movement Publications, 1997).

Ian T. Douglas has written a history of foreign mission in the Episcopal Church in *Fling Out the Banner: The National Church Ideal and the Foreign Mission of the Episcopal Church* (Church Hymnal, 1996).

⮑ Anglicanism

For a good overview of the history and theology of Anglicanism, see the revised edition of Stephen Sykes, John Booty, and Jonathan Knight's *The Study of Anglicanism* (SPCK/Fortress, 1998), which brings together thirty-one short essays on all aspects of Anglicanism by scholars from

America, England, Ireland, and Canada. Each essay begins with a short bibliography of relevant works in the field, so it is an indispensable reference tool for the student of Anglicanism.

Another valuable reference work is G. R. Evans and J. Robert Wright's *The Anglican Tradition* (SPCK/Fortress, 1991), which contains documents and texts from every period of Anglican history, beginning with the early church and ending with the ecumenical movement. Geoffrey Rowell has edited a collection of essays on leading English divines entitled *The English Religious Tradition and the Genius of Anglicanism* (IKON, 1992).

David L. Edwards sketches the theology of Anglicanism and important figures such as Jeremy Taylor and F. D. Maurice; see *What Anglicans Believe* (Forward Movement Publications, 1996). *The Spirit of Anglicanism*, edited by William J. Wolf (Morehouse, 1979), provides essays on Richard Hooker, F. D. Maurice, and William Temple. *The Spirit of the Oxford Movement: Tractarian Essays* by Owen Chadwick (Cambridge University Press, 1995) gives an overview of the Oxford Movement and the high church tradition as well as primary sources. Bernard M. G. Reardon has published a useful and larger study of the leading English religious leaders and movements in the nineteenth century entitled *Religious Thought in the Victorian Age: A Survey from Coleridge to Gore*, 2nd ed. (Longman, 1995). Included in this study are chapters on Coleridge, the Oxford Movement, F. D. Maurice, John Henry Newman, science and philosophy, developments in Scotland, and what Reardon calls "Critical Orthodoxy."

Another useful reference in this area is William T. Sachs' *The Transformation of Anglicanism: From State Church to Global Communion* (Cambridge University Press, 1993). As we look to the future of Anglicanism and the Anglican

Communion, an excellent resource is Mark Harris' *The Challenge of Change: The Anglican Communion in the Post-Modern Era* (Church Publishing, 1998).

～ Anglican Social Witness

Any list of resources on Anglican social witness would be incomplete without Archbishop William Temple's classic *Christianity and Social Order*, first published in 1942 (Shepheard-Walwyn, 1987). Robert Hood's *Social Teachings in the Episcopal Church* (Morehouse, 1990) provides an overview of Anglicanism's social theology and witness in the areas of war and peace, race, family life and sexuality, and economics. Paul T. Phillips' *A Kingdom on Earth: Anglo-American Social Christianity, 1880-1940* (Pennsylvania State University Press, 1996) provides a history of the Social Gospel and Christian Socialist movements in Britain, Canada, and the United States.

Bill Wylie Kellermann has edited an excellent volume on the witness of William Stringfellow entitled *Keeper of the Word: Selected Writings of William Stringfellow* (Eerdmans, 1994). Brian Grieves has edited and narrated a volume of sermons and addresses by Edmond Browning entitled *No Outcasts: The Public Witness of Edmond L. Browning, XXIVth Presiding Bishop of The Episcopal Church* (Forward Movement Publications, 1997). This compilation focuses on Browning's social witness with regard to the complicated issues facing the church in this age.

Little contemporary work has been done on the Episcopal Church and race, although Holmes' *A Brief History* describes the Civil War period. Harold T. Lewis' *Yet With a Steady Beat* (Trinity Press International, 1996) is an excellent and comprehensive treatment of the history of black Episcopalians, while Gardiner H. Shattuck's *Dwelling Together in Unity: Episcopalians and the Dilemmas of Race* (University Press of Kentucky, forthcoming) examines racial attitudes in the Episcopal Church from the Civil War period through the waning of the civil rights movement in the 1970s.

～ Anglican Devotional Writers

J. Robert Wright's *Prayer Book Spirituality* (Church Hymnal, 1989) is an interesting and useful collection of devotional writings on prayer, the church year, and the sacraments from classical Anglican sources, including Richard Hooker, George Herbert, and John Henry Hobart.

The Paulist Press series, *Classics of Western Spirituality*, provides good introductions to a number of Anglican devotional writers including the Caroline divines, and these have short biographies, good samplings, and excellent scholarly notes. See John Booty's *John Donne* (1990), John Wall's *George Herbert* (1981), Thomas K. Carroll's *Jeremy Taylor* (1990), P. G. Stanwood and Austin Warren's edition of William Law's *A Serious Call to a Devout and Holy Life* (1978), and Frank Whaling's edition of John and Charles Wesley's *Selected Prayers, Hymns, Journals, Notes, Sermons, Letters, and Treatises* (1981).

Works by Evelyn Underhill include *Evelyn Underhill: Modern Guide to the Quest for the Holy* (State University of New York Press, 1988) edited with an introduction by Dana Greene. A recent edition of Underhill's classic, *The Life of the Spirit and the Life of Today* (Morehouse, 1994) is edited by Susan Howatch in the Library of Anglican Spirituality.

For the life and writings of Thomas Traherne, see his *Centuries* (Harper, 1960), introduced by John Ferrar, and *Selections from Thomas Traherne's Centuries of Meditations*, edited with an introductory essay by William J. Wolf (Forward Movement Publications, 1980). See also Graham

Dowell's study *Enjoying the World: The Rediscovery of Thomas Traherne* (Mowbray, 1990).

While they do not represent "Anglican" writing in the usual sense, the devotional writings of Julian of Norwich and Hildegard of Bingen are influential in the English tradition. Julian's *Revelation of Divine Love*, edited and translated by John Skinner (Doubleday, 1996), is a good introduction to her thought. Fiona Bowie and Oliver Davies have edited *Hildegard of Bingen: An Anthology* (SPCK, 1990) which provides a useful entry into Hildegard's work.

The *Oxford Book of Seventeenth Century Verse* (Oxford University Press, 1992) and *The Oxford Book of Mystical Verse* (Clarendon Press, 1917) are also excellent resources for devotion.

Audiovisual Resources

A wide variety of videotapes are available to supplement a study of the history and theology of Anglicanism. The Center for the Ministry of Teaching at Virginia Theological Seminary (3737 Seminary Road, Alexandria, VA 22304) has a library of audio and video resources available to parishes.

Another excellent resource is provided by The Episcopal Radio/TV Foundation, which has audiocassettes and videotapes for purchase or rental. Their Anglican section includes material by a wide variety of Anglicans, including John Westerhoff, John Stott, Robert Runcie, and George Carey. Videotapes that could be used in conjunction with this book include topics such as the Anglican tradition, the Apostles' Creed, the Oxford Movement, and the Episcopal Church's mission to the western frontier. See especially the two-part video series, *The Story of the Episcopal Church* (Cathedral Films and Video) and the three-part video series, *The Story of Anglicanism* (Cathedral Films and Video).

Questions for Discussion

~ **Chapter 1: Living with History**

1. If you spent time in a church as a child, what strong memories do you have of people you loved, songs you liked to sing, customs you cherished? What faces, traditions, sights, smells, sounds, and tastes are part of your religious history? What customs, traditions, and activities caught your interest?

If you were not raised in a church, what memories do you have of religious traditions as a child? Who or what first attracted you to the church as an adult? What occasions drew you to become involved? What customs, traditions, and activities caught your interest?

2. How would you answer the question posed in this chapter, "How does tradition inform and shape our continuing witness as contemporary Christians?" What traditions do you think are most important for the church to uphold today? What traditions need to be reevaluated in the light of current understandings and practices?

∼ Chapter 2: Ten Touchstones of History

1. Discuss the author's invitation at the beginning of this chapter to consider your own "top ten" list of touchstones in history. How would you change her list to make it your own? Starting with your own perspective and experience, what historical moments, people, touchstones, or events do you especially remember? What struggles, tragedies, and joys have shaped your religious journey?

2. In your reading about the history of Christianity and, more specifically, Anglican and Episcopal history, what stands out for you as decisive? Which ancestors or achievements do you particularly value? Why? What do they teach you about living your faith in the present?

∼ Chapter 3: The Ministry We Share

1. During the week find a quiet opportunity to read and reflect on 1 Corinthians 12. How does Paul envision ministry in the body of Christ? How are the spiritual gifts described here reflected in your congregation? Are some of the gifts missing? If so, what effect does that have on the life of the parish?

2. When you hear the word "minister," do you think of ordinary Christians living out their faith in society at large? What does the term "people of God" mean to you? In what ways do you think the church acknowledges the ministries of lay people in the church? in the world? Do you think of yourself as a minister in the church?

3. Read the sections in the Catechism on "The Church" and "The Ministry" (BCP 854–856). Would you have answered the questions in the same way? How would you answer them differently, based on your experience of the church?

What other questions about the church and the ministry do you have?

～ Chapter 4: Living with Controversy

1. Can you think of an occasion in your life when information from the past helped you face a difficult choice between alternatives in the present? How did that historical knowledge inform your decision?

2. What are some of the issues causing conflict and controversy in the church today? in your parish? How are the people involved dealing with them?

3. How could the three historical approaches to conflict described in this chapter—compromise, denial, and integration of new knowledge—apply to various conflicts and controversies in the church today?

～ Chapter 5: Recycling Tradition

1. Have you found yourself reflecting upon your relationship to creation during worship with your congregation? Where in the celebration of the Holy Eucharist or in Morning Prayer are you drawn to think about your relationship to creation? Are there particular hymns or prayers that reveal to you something of God in creation?

2. What new issues are of pressing concern in our world today other than the environmental crisis? What do you think the role of church tradition could be in addressing these concerns? How could a deepened understanding of church history prove helpful? If these concerns were not directly anticipated by our Christian ancestors, what parallels can you see in how they dealt with similar concerns?

⁓ **Chapter 6: New Occasions Teach New Duties**

1. Do you think of yourself as an active part of history? If so, how? If not, why not? What would need to change in order for you to think of yourself in that way?

2. Read Article XXXIV, "Of the Traditions of the Church," of the Thirty-Nine Articles, found on page 874 of the *Book of Common Prayer*. How might this article speak to the questions and disagreements in church life today?

3. How would you respond to the author's question at the end of the chapter, "Is the Episcopal Church a traditional church?" How has your response changed as a result of reading and discussing this book?